Property of Acacia Village

Library

Given by:

Helen

Squire

In Memory of:

....

....

Date: Aug. 15, 2004

Helen —

Merry Christmas!

Jack

— Christmas '99

D1187478

RETURN TO
ACACIA VILLAGE LIBRARY
A CARING COMMUNITY
UTICA, N.Y. 13501

RETURN TO
ACACIA VILLAGE LIBRARY
A MASONIC COMMUNITY
UTICA, N.Y. 13501

◦⇒ Early Days in the Adirondacks ⇐◦

THE PHOTOGRAPHS OF SENECA RAY STODDARD

Tupper Lake from Bog River Falls

2

Schroon Lake, seen looking south from the Leland House

Au Sable Pass from Beede House, a hotel for sportsmen

Echo Camp at Raquette Lake. Phineas Lounsbury, a governor of Connecticut, had this camp built for him by the Adirondack developer William West Durant in the early 1880s.

Hotel Ampersand at Saranac Lake

Mount Marcy, from Keene Valley

The Giant. *Keene Valley*

The Guide House at Paul Smith's hotel at St. Regis Lake, which maintained a resident staff of guides, along with a fleet of guideboats.

Stoddard captioned this, "The way it looks from the stern seat."

Untitled

12

Early Days in the
ADIRONDACKS

The Photographs of
SENECA RAY STODDARD

by Jeanne Winston Adler

Foreword by John Wilmerding

HARRY N. ABRAMS, INC., PUBLISHERS

For my parents, Gordon and Katharine Willey

(Page 14) Untitled (Self-Portrait?) Seneca Ray Stoddard in his twenties

EDITOR: Robert Morton
EDITORIAL ASSISTANT: Nola Butler
DESIGNER: Dana Sloan

Library of Congress Cataloging-in-Publication Data
Stoddard, Seneca Ray, 1844–1917.
     Early days in the Adirondacks : the photographs of Seneca Ray Stoddard /
  by Jeanne Winston Adler.
       p.   cm.
     Includes bibliographical references and index.
     ISBN 0–8109–0897–2 (clothbound)
      1. Adirondack Mountains (N.Y.)–History–Pictorial works.
  2. Landscape–New York (State)–Adirondack Mountains–Pictorial works.
  3. Landscape photography–New York (State)–Adirondack Mountains.
  4. Stoddard, Seneca Ray, 1844–1917–Biography. 5. Photographers–New
  York (State)–Adirondack Mountains–Biography.
  I. Adler, Jeanne Winston, 1946– . II. Title.
  F127.A2S764 1997
  974.7'5041–dc21   97-4304

Copyright © 1997 Jeanne Winston Adler

Published in 1997 by Harry N. Abrams, Incorporated, New York
All rights reserved. No part of the contents of this book may be reproduced
without the written permission of the publisher
Printed and bound in Japan

Harry N. Abrams, Inc.
100 Fifth Avenue
New York, N.Y. 10011
www.abramsbooks.com

CONTENTS

At Martin's, Saranac Lake, September 21, 1876

PREFACE

Seneca Ray Stoddard's studio on Elm Street in Glens Falls, New York, staffed by his wife and other women assistants, turned out thousands of prints over his long career, which lasted from the late 1860s into the first years of the twentieth century. Many of these prints, used on postcards and in books of views, were of poor quality.

Fortunately, in 1877 and again during the years 1888–91, Stoddard sent numbers of fine prints to the U.S. Copyright Office in Washington, D.C. Also, sometime after his death in 1917, Bertha Stoddard, the wife of a nephew, rescued some of the contents of the Elm Street studio and preserved the material in her own home on Pine Street in Glens Falls.

In 1962, Maitland De Sormo, an Adirondack native and writer on Adirondack history, acquired the bulk of this material with the idea of using the photographs to illustrate a book. He eventually made use of the photographs for several books – incidentally providing a strange visual experience for his readers. The Stoddard photographs fill the early portions of the books and then give way to more recent photographs chosen to illustrate chapters on twentieth-century events. Abruptly, the Adirondack scenes lose their intensity and much of their beauty. Without knowing why, the reader has a strong impression that the mountains and lakes have deteriorated in recent years.

De Sormo, who wrote a biography of Stoddard in 1967, became a champion of the photographer. (In some ways, De Sormo resembled Stoddard. Both had lived on the harsh, northern edge of the Adirondacks in Franklin County – in locations not ten miles distant. Both were highly independent, inventive people with a keen eye for business.) De Sormo sold some of the prints and other items acquired from Bertha Stoddard to private collectors; most he divided between two institutions, the Chapman Historical Museum in Glens Falls and the Adirondack Museum in Blue Mountain Lake.

The Chapman Historical Museum holds approximately 7,000 Stoddard prints, the Adirondack Museum approximately 5,000. Very many of these are duplicates, but the museum collections still represent a tremendous body of work, and contain hundreds of fine prints.

In the Adirondacks. *The man at the right is Charles Oblenis, Stoddard's brother-in-law.*

FOREWORD:
The Photographic Eye of Seneca Ray Stoddard

by John Wilmerding

The phrase "to have an eye" suggests more than the mere faculty of seeing with a discriminating sense of perception, with a fine-tuned intellectual faculty for aesthetic refinement and point of view. Seneca Ray Stoddard (1843–1917) developed such an eye as a prolific and celebrated landscape photographer during the great period of that medium's early maturity and of American nature as a central preoccupation for our country's artists in the last half of the nineteenth century. While one of his continuing passions was the documentation of the leisure life associated with wilderness trails, roads, and lakeside resorts throughout the Adirondack region of upstate New York, he also found the time and inclination to compose more pure landscape views of careful structure and great clarity. Many of these are sensitively selected views of mountain valleys or distant ranges suffused in hazy light or sharply reflected in mirrored expanses of lake surfaces. The best of his work may now be seen to take an estimable place alongside the landscape paintings of the later Hudson River School and luminist painters, sharing with them an overriding concern for the myriad textures of nature and the poetic effects of light and atmosphere.

Stoddard was born in Wilton, Saratoga County, New York, and while he would eventually travel widely in his photographic work, the picturesque glories of his native region stand as the central achievement of his career. Versatile as a painter, writer, and editor, Stoddard in his maturity was well recognized for his artistic photography. With a modest education in rural schools and an early apprenticeship as a decorative painter, it is believed he largely taught himself the rudiments of photography, making his first significant pictures of Au Sable Chasm in the 1860s. During the following decade he produced an important series of guidebooks to the major scenic areas of Saratoga Springs, Lakes George and Champlain, and the Adirondack mountains; paralleling these was the publication in 1873 of his first concentrated group of pictures in *The Adirondacks Illustrated*. During the eighties, with sustained energies and ambition he undertook a canoe trip over several summers along the Atlantic coast from Long Island to Nova Scotia, and in the 1890s ventured even farther to photograph in Alaska, Florida, the American West, and the Mediterranean.

Stoddard's Adirondack work begins at a time of the later stages of Hudson River painting, when pictorial attention was shifting from the intense recording of nature's foreground details to the broader vistas of distant space and sun-flooded panoramas. As such, his style is at once indebted to the earlier artistic conventions of densely framed views and meticulously rendered details as well as to the emerging luminosity and spiritual contemplation of American landscape art during the third quarter of the nineteenth century. Among those of the first generation of Adirondack photographers, who just preceded Stoddard, perhaps most representative is William J. Stillman (1828–1901), whose work was given its first comprehensive treatment in the 1988 exhibition and publication by Anne Ehrenkranz et al., *Poetic Localities: Photographs of William J. Stillman*. Almost a generation older than Stoddard, Stillman was also a native of upstate New York, born in Schenectady, and likewise began as a landscape painter, later taking up writing and editing. Perhaps best known as the founder and first editor of *The Crayon* in 1855, he counted among his close friends such key cultural figures of his age as Ralph Waldo Emerson, Charles Eliot Norton, Louis Agassiz, John Ruskin, and D. G. Rossetti. In another predictive parallel to Stoddard, after his early photography in the Adirondacks, Stillman also went abroad and produced an important body of photographs at several sites in the Mediterranean. Close to the Hudson River painters Asher Durand and Frederick Church at midcentury, he took his first Adirondack photographs in 1859. A few years earlier Stillman had spent a winter in the woods, and an extensive 1857 camping trip through the Adirondacks with James Russell Lowell to Tupper, Raquette, and Upper Saranac lakes led to the formation of the Adirondack Club by several illustrious Bostonians.

In contrast to Stoddard's images of the next decades, Stillman's prints were indebted to the analytic spirit of Durand's and Ruskin's meticulous exploration and recording of nature's organic details. His images were strongly composed, favoring close-range views of the woodland ground at our feet, with sharp differentiation of grass, fern, and tree types. Stoddard instead would seem to raise his angle of vision to look farther in the middle and far distance and to exploit more the expressive elements of open skies and bathing sunlight. His views occupy a stylistic and chronological middle ground between Stillman's Ruskinian approach and the later abstracted and luminist manners of, for example, the New England photographer Henry L. Rand (1862–1945). Perhaps the first broad exposure to a selection of Stoddard's best prints occurred with the sweeping exhibition of luminist painting and graphics in 1980, the National Gallery's *American Light: The Luminist Movement, 1850–1875*. Here the formal affinities of his photographs with those of contemporary painters like John F. Kensett and Martin Johnson Heade became apparent. Considered in this larger stylistic context, Stoddard's images are revealing for their mixture of documentary and poetic elements, concern with the physical as well as contemplative aspects of nature, and balance of explicit details with broad light effects.

When Stoddard first began photographing in the Lake George area, and in particular the striking rock formation of Au Sable Chasm, during the 1860s, he was following in the footsteps of William Stillman and joined by other photographers like George Barker and G. E. Curtis, along with such painters as Kensett and David Johnson. Indeed, Stoddard shares with the latter the penchant for strongly horizontal compositions, often balancing rocky outcroppings on one side with glassy open lake water on the other. Au Sable Chasm itself he described as "a little depression in the otherwise level country, a wooded valley with gently sloping slides . . . the site of this grand wonder – a Yosemite in miniature." This attitude of celebration in prose and print was characteristic of the period, and Stoddard's records of place at their best have an elevated and distilled sense of nature's purest moments. During his extensive wilderness excursions he frequently sought spacious light-filled views, which he managed to capture in balanced and harmonious compositions. Exhilarated before a special prospect, such as those around Lake George, he could recall "the wonderful beauty of the day, the clear, crisp atmosphere surrounding us – the great purple-rimmed basin, in the center of which, lifted up on a pinnacle, we stood, while the mighty, sweeping dome of heaven came down all around and blended with the mountain edges."

In his most memorable works Stoddard displayed a refined command of different textures and tonalities, with a focus on strongly outlined forms and the skillful use of sharp reflections. Characteristic of both his stylistic variety and strength are such photographs as *Buttermilk Falls near Deerland*, with its three major horizontal zones, the foamy lacework center and surrounding animated details; *Drowned Lands on the Raquette River near Tupper Lake*, with its spiky dead trees silhouetted against the sky in an image of nature's renewal going back to Thomas Cole's early Hudson River paintings in the 1820s; or *Guide House at Paul Smith's*, composed with the interlocking rhythmic shapes of canoes, shed door openings, and human figures. Later, during the 1880s, when Stoddard reached Mount Desert Island on the Maine coast in his sailing canoe *Atlantis*, he made carefully observed photographs of the rocky shore and seaweed as well as of the cog railway then rising to the highest summit of Green Mountain. There he joined in the grand artistic tradition of numerous American painters who had exulted in Maine's scenery as viewed from its prominent mountain peaks and slopes over preceding decades, including Cole in the 1840s, Fitz Hugh Lane and Frederick Church in the fifties, Sanford Gifford in the sixties, and Alfred Thomas Bricher in the seventies. Stoddard could have spoken for them all when he proclaimed, "It was glorious up there! Nature had done much for the place. The view was superb, the air wonderful, the sunset most beautiful, the sunrise glorious and the great star-studded concave, stooping downward at night, made heaven itself seem near." Even later, near the end of the century, Stoddard photographed Indian life and territories in northwest Canada and Alaska with a stark poignancy close in spirit to the work of Edward Curtis at the same time. But in all of Stoddard's work one feels a driving impulse of preservation, to save and savor a particular realm or experience in nature, to record a favored scene indelibly for himself and for posterity. Now in the late twentieth century, when the Adirondack wilderness is under the danger of encroachment, we can doubly appreciate Stoddard's art for what it preserved from his time to ours and may help save for the future.

ACKNOWLEDGMENTS

My thanks go first of all to those who provided the photographs for this book: the Chapman Historical Museum, Glens Falls, N.Y.; the Adirondack Museum, Blue Mountain Lake, N.Y.; the Howard Greenberg Gallery, New York, N.Y.; With Pipe and Book, Lake Placid, N.Y.; and Albert Gates, Moriah, N.Y. Both former and present directors of the Chapman Historical Museum, John Polnak and Lisa Simpson, and former and present curators, Beth Shepard and Lori Fisher, supplied help above and beyond the call of duty in the preparation of this book. At the Adirondack Museum, Jackie Day, Director, Jim Meehan, Curator of Photography, and Jerold Pepper, Librarian, gave the same kind of generous help. My special thanks to Jim Meehan for his explanations of the technical processes of Stoddard's photography and for his reading of the book in manuscript. Special thanks also to Albert Gates for sharing with me his knowledge of the photographer; to Breck Turner of With Pipe and Book for allowing me to view his library of rare Adirondack materials; and to Howard Greenberg for pointing out one important photograph that I had overlooked.

Much of the research for this book was done in local history archives and libraries. I would like to thank Stacey Draper of the Rennselaer County Historical Society for sharing her knowledge of Troy painters, the members of the Franklin County Historical Society for their help in tracing the Stoddard family in Burke, in particular Beth Brand, Town Clerk of Burke, who pinpointed the Hawk's Hollow site of the Stoddard family farm; Lorraine Westcott, Town Historian of Wilton, who provided me with her research on the Stoddard family in Wilton; Dorothy Alsdorf of the Saratoga County Historical Society; and the curators of the Brookside Museum, Ballston Spa, N.Y.

I also leaned heavily upon the services of the reference librarians of the Crandall Library, Glens Falls, N.Y. (particular thanks to Bruce Cole, who also read the book in manuscript); the New York State Library, Albany, N.Y.; the Troy and Albany public libraries; and the Albany Institute of History and Art.

The opportunity to meet and speak at length with Ernestine Stoddard, great-niece of the photographer, and Maitland De Sormo, Stoddard's first biographer, was one of the great pleasures of my research. I valued these meetings very much, and they inspired me to look more deeply for the inner man, the personality of my subject.

I must also acknowledge the help of Nathan Farb, one of the most devoted modern-day photographers of the Adirondacks, at the outset of this project, and that of Joseph Cutshall King, a former director of the Chapman Historical Museum, in its later stages. Farb gave me the benefit of his views on Stoddard and his work; Cutshall King provided me with research on Stoddard in Glens Falls as well as much information on the Chapman Historical Museum's Stoddard Collection.

Finally, warm thanks to Andrew Stewart for his help in introducing this book to the publisher; to Michael Bogin, Professor of Art, Hobart College, Geneva, N.Y., for his analysis of Stoddard's painting; to Howard Kirschenbaum, Camp Uncas, Raquette Lake, N.Y., for some vital bits of Adirondack information; to my editor, Robert Morton, and his assistant, Nola Butler, for their skillful rearrangement of chapters and paragraphs; and to my husband, Jeffrey Adler, who encouraged me to write about a photographer he has long admired.

The Raquette River at Sweeney Carry

INTRODUCTION

Seneca Ray Stoddard (1843–1917) belongs to the heroic age of American landscape photography, the era of the great western photographers, Timothy H. O'Sullivan, William Henry Jackson, A. J. Russell, Carleton E. Watkins, and Eadweard Muybridge. Stoddard did not work in the West until late in his career and then only very briefly. He is, quintessentially, the photographer of the eastern wilderness, the Adirondacks, which were opening up to travelers and sportsmen only in the mid-nineteenth century.

Stoddard's career parallels those of some western contemporaries. Like them, he served on government survey expeditions and took commissions from railway companies opening lines into newly explored regions. He employed the same materials and formats for his photographs. Why, then, is Stoddard so little known compared with his western colleagues? For one thing, many of his prints lay undiscovered in Glens Falls, New York, until the 1960s. But it is also true that Stoddard's subject matter – the eastern wilderness landscape – has a powerful association with the long-out-of-favor Hudson River School painters and their immediate successors. The western photographers also came out of the Hudson River landscape tradition, but their canvas – the dramatic, new terrain of the West – put some distance between their work and that of the army of artists who painted along the Hudson and in the mountains of New York and New England from the 1830s through the 1880s and beyond.

In his day, however, Stoddard was fully as popular and successful as any of the western men. In addition to his landscapes, he produced other work: interiors and exteriors of hotels and private camps with guests posed on lawns or verandas, lumber camps and tuberculosis sanitariums with their inmates, campfire scenes of hunters and guides, as well as a number of fascinating portraits of Indians and blacks. Almost single-handedly, his photography documents the architecture and the social scene of a long-ago Adirondack world. These images have more than purely historical value. Stoddard's organizing vision of the world informs all of his work.

In 1980 art historian John Wilmerding, then a curator at the National Gallery of Art, Washington, included a number of Stoddard photographs in an exhibition of painting and photography called *American Light*, an exhibition that defined the style known as luminism. Drawing on a large collection of Stoddard prints that had been filed with the U.S. Copyright Office, Wilmerding identified the photographer as one of the artist/creators of this intensely native vision that was centered mainly in landscape painting.

Wilmerding wrote that the luminists' "interest in the radiant effects of light and atmosphere" resulted in "some of the most beautiful and compelling paintings ever executed in the history of American art." And Stoddard, according to Wilmerding, "took some of the purest luminist photographs we might find." Photohistorian Weston Naef, in a separate essay in the catalogue, reaffirmed Stoddard's important place among early American photographers.

In northern New York, Stoddard's name has a lingering fame, partly for his work as a photographer of the region, but equally for some other activities. He produced a series of guidebooks and maps of the area. He wrote and spoke on behalf of the creation of the Adirondack Park; in 1891, to lobby for the park bill, he presented his popular lantern slide lecture, "The Adirondacks Illustrated," before the New York Assembly.

Through the 1890s and the first years of this century, Stoddard probably enjoyed the greatest financial success of his career by touring the country and giving a variety of illustrated lectures. He photographed in the American West and South, in Alaska, Canada, Europe, and the Near East, and he presented views of all these places to lecture audiences.

But it is the photography made at Lake George, Lake Champlain, and in the Adirondacks that forms his masterwork (along with some images from the White Mountains of New Hampshire, the lower Hudson River, and the New England and Canadian seacoasts). These are the photographs of the 1870s and 1880s. During these years, Stoddard looked at the mountains, sky, lakes, habitations, and people of the wilderness regions of northern New York and saw something extraordinary there. He looked at them with a highly charged gaze that converted many views of real places into little glimpses of heaven. His vision also posed and illuminated people and objects in ways that invested them with a special, partly spiritual, meaning.

Where did this vision come from? The nineteenth-century world of ideas, and certain traditions of painting, formed Stoddard's eye in great part, but his own social and psychological experience also played a role. Exploring all this is like making a trip into the middle of the nineteenth century. What an exotic place the modern-day voyager finds there. People's lives, thoughts, and occupations followed completely different pathways just a century and a half ago. Even straightforward labels like artist and photogra-pher did not always mean the same then as now.

During the 1850s and 1860s Stoddard's world was beset by violence and flux. We learn that the beautiful and serene images he produced in the 1870s and 1880s come out of considerable intellectual, social, and personal struggles of those earlier decades. The old conflicts and passions have now faded, but a careful tracing of them provides the way into Stoddard's work.

This is probably a self-portrait made in Seneca Ray Stoddard's twenties.

The Roadside
Watering Trough

Chapter One
WILTON, BURKE, AND TROY

Seneca Ray Stoddard grew up in a world that was in the process of crumbling apart and reforming itself. As a result of this turmoil, what most called "progress," his parents suffered a lifetime of dislocation and saw their fortunes fall well below those of their own parents.

Stoddard was born May 13, 1843, in Wilton, New York, which lies about midway between Saratoga Springs and Glens Falls to the northeast. He was probably born in the house of his maternal grandfather, Roswell Ray, because town records show that his father, Charles Stoddard, was either absent from the town or landless from January 1843 until January 1848.

Charles Stoddard moved all the time; this was the single fact about him that his grandchildren could remember years later. Between 1837 – when he probably married Julia Ray – and 1842, he occupied four different farms in Wilton.

Whatever Charles Stoddard's movements in the mid-1840s, by 1848, he, Julia, and their three surviving children, Edward, aged ten, Seneca Ray, aged five, and Charles Stanley, aged two, all lived in the old Ray house at Dimick Corners in Wilton. (Another son, Charles Eugene, had died in 1844 at the age of three.)

Seneca Ray's mother, Julia, was the youngest of nine children of

Roswell and Leah Ray, longtime Wilton residents who may have both descended from Dutch settlers of the region. Roswell Ray, who died in 1844, was a Revolutionary War veteran, and his staunch Republicanism is the source of Seneca Ray Stoddard's first name. Seneca, the first-century Roman senator and opponent of the tyrants Nero and Caligula, appealed strongly to American patriots in the years after the French Revolution. Roswell Ray named his only son, born in 1798, Seneca. Forty-five years later, Julia Ray Stoddard named her son after this brother – although the name itself had fallen out of fashion by then.

On his father's side, Seneca Ray Stoddard descended from a distinguished New England family. A nineteenth-century genealogy, *Anthony Stoddard of Boston, Massachusetts, and His Descendants*, supplies a generation-by-generation outline linking Charles Stoddard and his father, Samuel, with a number of famous seventeenth- and eighteenth-century ministers. (Seneca Ray Stoddard owned a copy of this genealogy and also sent another copy to his son, LeRoy, in 1915.)[1]

Grandfather Samuel Stoddard, born in Woodbury, Connecticut, moved with other Woodbury families to the new town of Alford, Massachusetts, in the Berkshires about 1802. He ranked as an important man there, running for selectman in 1810 and for Berkshire County treasurer in 1821. He was probably a minister, as was his oldest surviving son, Parley (born in 1804).[2] It is worth noting that after Samuel left Alford for Saratoga County (between 1830 and 1833), a nephew who remained in the town went on to serve two terms in the Massachusetts Legislature (1842 and 1860).

In his late middle age, Samuel Stoddard moved into Saratoga County with his three youngest sons.

He was able to provide each of these late-born sons with an inheritance worth about $1,000 in 1850 money, enough to set them up as substantial artisan/farmers, although not enough to make them wealthy, full-time farmers. (Such men owned $3,000 to $4,000 worth of land in that time and place.)[3]

Charles's older brother John Stoddard, a shoemaker and farmer, became a respected and successful citizen of Moreau, the town that adjoins Wilton to the north. He twice served as Moreau tax assessor in the 1850s and had a net worth of over $4,000 in 1860. Charles Stoddard, however, could not make a settled place for himself in Saratoga County or, as it turned out, anywhere else. But he remained for a substantial portion of Seneca Ray's childhood – from 1848 at least through 1854 – at Dimick Corners in Wilton.

That part of Wilton is a foothill region of the Adirondacks; the Palmer Mountains, the southernmost spur of the Adirondacks, reach south into the town just a few miles west of Dimick Corners. From the empty lot where the Ray–Stoddard house once stood there is a good view of Mount McGregor, the highest peak of the Palmer range. Palmer Ridge Road, which leads north from Dimick Corners into Moreau, parallels a section of the mountain chain and offers a vista of the whole spur, stretched out like a long blue cliff beyond open fields.

In the 1840s and 1850s the neighborhood looked north to the Adirondack forests for part of its living. A number of area men worked at getting out lumber on French Mountain, around Lake George, and in other nearby sections of the Adirondacks.[4] At that time, Dimick Corners approached the size of a village. *Samuel Geil's 1856 Map of Saratoga County* shows eighteen houses there, counting those that straggle west on the Gansevoort–Wilton Road a quarter of a mile, and south along Dimick Road for the same distance. There was a schoolhouse, School No. 3, though no regular meetinghouse. Residents traveled a mile south to Emerson's Corners to attend a "Union" church shared (in sequence) by Methodists, Baptists, and Presbyterians.

Wilton was a web of populous villages during these pre–Civil War years. Doe's Corners, with more than two dozen houses, several stores, a hotel, and Wilton Academy, lay two miles west of Dimick Corners on the Gansevoort–Wilton Road. Two miles to the east was the village of Gansevoort, with as many houses as Doe's Corners, a cluster of grist and textile mills, and a station of the Saratoga and Rennselaer Railroad line, which ran from Saratoga Springs to Whitehall, New York.

At Dimick Corners, the Stoddards lived next door to a carpenter, Daniel Wait, who served as a witness to Julia's will and also testified on Charles Stoddard's behalf in a minor law case.[5] His presence underlines the fact that Seneca Ray Stoddard grew up in a world of craftsmen: tanners, curriers, shoemakers, saddlers, coopers, cabinetmakers, masons, blacksmiths, painters, chairmakers, wagonmakers, and others. Their workshops were everywhere in that busy countryside. Charles Stoddard's own trade or business is unknown, probably because he didn't follow it with much success.

Charles's difficulties may have been partly personal ones, but not entirely. Paradoxically, the nation's boom and growth of the 1840s and 1850s brought depression to most of the countryside in settled areas of New England and New York. People simply drained off to the new western lands and to the new industrial cities. At the same time, increasing quantities of mass-produced goods struck at the livelihoods of traditional craftsmen.

On closer examination, what was described as the "busy countryside" of Wilton looks distressed and turbulent. Epidemics of disease, probably spread from the boatloads of immigrants traveling the Champlain Canal and the Hudson, swept through the region in 1832, 1844, and 1849. In 1849 an epidemic of smallpox in the spring was followed by one of cholera in the summer. Perhaps in reaction, the town experienced major religious revivals in 1839, 1842, and 1850. A Methodist minister, Abel Ford, who lived only yards from the Stoddard household at Dimick Corners, led a revival in 1850, which must have had a strong impact on the Methodist Stoddards.

Against this backdrop of hard times, Julia Stoddard died in the summer of 1851, shortly after the birth of her fifth child. Charles remarried within months of her death, and in 1854 he sold his Wilton property and moved his family north, perhaps into Washington County for a time, and ultimately to Franklin County in the extreme northern part of New York State.[6]

Charles lived for at least one year, 1860, at Hawk's Hollow in the town of Burke, Franklin County.[7] Like Dimick Corners, Hawk's Hollow is located on the fringes of the Adirondack region, but just out of sight of the mountains to the south. A swift-running branch of the Trout River runs down from the high land just west of Little Chateaugay Lake and cuts through the hollow on its way north.

In the nineteenth century, Hawk's Hollow was much the same kind of place as Dimick Corners. Both were populated with farmer-artisans, and both were strongly Methodist. Some of the inhabitants may have literally been the same people: in 1850 the owner of the Hawk's Hollow sawmill was one Walter Dimick.

A census report of June 1860 reports that in the Stoddard household Seneca Ray, aged seventeen, had attended school for some part of the previous year.[5] But he may have also begun formal or informal training as a decorative painter. About a mile up the Trout River from Hawk's Hollow, a painter and carriagemaker named Hiram Cartwright had a large shop in Burke Hollow. Burke Hollow boasted a number of small industries at this period: a foundry that produced stoves, a tannery, a starch factory (potatoes were the raw material), and several other mills. But Burke, like Wilton, had already reached the high point of its growth. Population declined after 1860, and almost all the Burke Hollow industries were gone within another generation. It was undergoing the same kind of painful shrinkage – ten years on – as Wilton.

At the start of the Civil War, on July 4, 1861, a violent protest took place in Burke Hollow that reveals the anger and desperation of some Burke townsmen at this time. The skilled craftsman Hiram Cartwright, who emerges as the likely candidate as Stoddard's first painting instructor, was the main actor in the affair. Frederick Seaver, a local historian, recounted in *Historical Sketches of Franklin County*:

> *Hiram Cartwright and other sympathizers raised a secession flag at the Hollow. The flag had been painted by William Hollenbeck. The time was when the Hollow was deemed one of the hardest places in the county, and the day was doubtless the wildest that Burke ever knew. It is said that there were two hundred men drunk there on that day, and drunk in*

no ordinary degree, but ravingly so. The men who were back of the flag raising armed themselves, assembled at the foot of the pole, and declared that they would shoot any one who should attempt to haul down the flag. Word of the affair reached Malone, and a company of sober men, quite as thoroughly in earnest as the rabble at Burke, was recruited, largely from the railroad machine shops, to go to Burke for the purpose of tearing down the rag....

The Stoddards did not witness this wild day; they had already moved on. Charles had reason to try and better his fortunes elsewhere. He hadn't prospered like his older brother, John, and possessed an estate valued at less than $1,500 in 1860.

The family did not go west – not yet – but south again into or near the industrial hub surrounding the city of Troy, New York.[9] In 1862, Seneca Ray Stoddard began work as an ornamental painter at the Gilbert Car Company on Green Island, Watervliet, where he remained through the spring of 1864. Gilbert's manufactured railway engines and coaches and employed a whole department of painters to decorate its passenger cars with landscape scenes and other types of painting.

Green Island and the village of Watervliet on the west bank of the Hudson really functioned as parts of Troy. In fact, Watervliet was generally known as West Troy during the 1850s and 1860s. Iron and steel mills powered the tremendous growth of this greater Troy area at midcentury, when the population of Troy proper went from approximately 11,000 persons in 1830 to 39,000 in 1860. Most of the newcomers were immigrants; by 1860, three out of five Troy residents were foreign-born, the great majority coming from Ireland.

Green Island lies at the geographic center of the industrial sprawl that still lines both sides of the river here. The island is flat and low-lying; from many points there is a feeling of standing at the bottom of a cup with the higher ground of the mainland areas – particularly Troy on the east bank – rising up in the near distance.

Stoddard, coming from an upland farming village, surely experienced the place as a kind of industrial caldron. By 1860, Green Island was the site of three foundries, a railroad machine shop, and the Gilbert Car factory, whose works covered several acres in the center of the island. Some striking descriptions of foundries and the metalworking process from Stoddard's later writings point to the effect such scenes had on his imagination. Though Stoddard wrote the following passages about the ironworks at Clinton Prison in Auburn, New York, he clearly found huge, industrial workplaces such as those on Green Island exciting, but unnatural, environments:

the high fence shut off the view, but between the chinks we could see flashing lights, the glow of fires on the chimney tops, could hear the hiss of steam, the labored breathing of the huge blowers and that indescribable sound which no musical term expresses, of the great trip hammer descending first on the soft mass of glowing fire that sheds tears of blood and gradually shrinks and hardens until we hear the clear ring of the metals battling with each other . . . the blackened beams and rafters overhead, great heaps of coal, piled up masses of iron, huge bars and rods bent and twisted, the massive trip hammer seeming to act and think with an intelligence of its own, great cylinders which fed with shining bars of iron, shot them out in long squirming lines of fire,

writhing bands that in endless revolutions leaped up into the unknown regions above . . . roaring of the fires, the hiss of steam, the hoarse breathing of the blowers, the splash and drip of water sent against the smoking roof and sides. Shadowy forms in human shape, now feeding the hungry furnaces, now shielding their faces, with iron bars they excite the fierce flames to fiercer wrath, now struggling forward and past with bodies of unknown matter.[10]

Stoddard's sojourn in Troy occurred during the middle of an important period of struggle for the city. Between 1850 and 1880, Troy's largely immigrant work force battled mill owners for control of the workplace. The workers lost in the end. Wages fell, and the Troy ironmasters – helped by changes in modes of production – asserted company rule over all matters of hiring, firing, and skill requirements. They pushed the ironworkers, who were once highly paid, skilled craftsmen, closer to the status of industrial operatives.

But during the early 1860s, this outcome lay in the future. If anything, the cause of the workers appeared to be on the upswing. The iron molders struck successfully in the spring and summer of 1861 and again in the spring of 1864. Between these dates Troy experienced two major disasters: the greatest fire of its history in May 1862, and a three-day riot in July of 1863. Stoddard witnessed repeated scenes of public disorder during his time on Green Island.

The fire exploded from a railroad accident on the bridge that connected Green Island with Troy; fire blew the flames up the hill to burn an eight-block section of the city. The riot began in Troy proper with a procession of workingmen, who gathered to protest the new draft law of this midpoint year in the 1861–65 Civil War. It soon carried over into West Troy, where the mostly Irish mobs attacked the Watervliet Arsenal, and only armed men stationed on the roofs of all the buildings repelled them. Mobs also terrorized the city's African-American population – the very source and cause of the war in the rioters' view – and blacks fled in large numbers to the woods near West Troy.

While these civic traumas played out, alongside the national trauma of the Civil War, Troy enjoyed the last years of a remarkably rich art scene. The city supported a distinguished portrait painter, Abel Buell Moore, whose works divide neatly into portraits with severe, linear faces, done before his European tour, and those with rosy, rounded faces done afterward. William Richardson Tyler, a one-time painter at the Gilbert Car factory, maintained a gallery on River Street together with another painter, Bradley Bucklin, and a sculptor, Tom Wallace. Tyler specialized in landscape and marine views and exhibited at least once at the National Academy of Design in New York City.

But these men represented only a fraction of the artistic life of the city. The city's manufacturers actively patronized the work of the foremost painters of the day, who were in large part native artists in the sense that many had been born and/or trained within a thirty-mile radius of Troy. These men increasingly migrated to studio buildings in New York City for the winter months. The growing commercial power of New York City, plus its two new art associations, the National Academy and the American Art Union, had tremendously expanded the opportunities for artists there. Still, the Hudson River painters retained important links, at least with patrons, in Troy.

Between 1858 and 1862, civic leaders (mostly the iron manufacturers) mounted five public art exhibitions at the Troy Young Men's Association. Judging by the catalogue of the 1862 winter exhibition, these shows featured the works of almost every notable Hudson River artist. The 1862 catalogue lists 123 oils plus a quantity of watercolors owned by Troy citizens, except those that came directly from the artists' studios, as well as a sprinkling of works from the collection of the YMA itself, and from that of a local gallery and jewelry store, Sims. The 1862 exhibit displayed five works or more by each of the following artists: Frederick Church, Jervis McEntee, Sanford Gifford, William Hart, William Richardson Tyler, and Homer Martin. Excepting Tyler and Martin, these men maintained studios in New York City. But Church owned property in Hudson just fifteen miles south of Troy (where he would eventually build his Moorish-style villa, Olana); Gifford's family lived in Hudson; and William Hart was a graduate, like Tyler, of the ornamental painting department of Troy's Gilbert Car Company. Hart also maintained strong connections in nearby Albany. McEntee, who has no clear connection with Troy, may have found patrons there through his former teacher, Church. Tyler was a Troy artist who continued to work in the city almost until his death in 1896. Homer Martin, a student of both William Hart and his brother James Hart (another Gilbert alumnus), lived and worked in nearby Albany through 1862.

Another Troy artist, D. W. C. Boutelle, who reportedly left the city in 1846, supplied only a single painting for the 1862 YMA show, but the association chose to purchase this painting along with a handful of others for its permanent collection.

To some extent, the YMA followed in the footsteps of the American Art Union of New York City. Each season, this organization of artists and "merchant-amateurs" commissioned dozens of expensive artworks from painters and sculptors and then sold lottery chances on them. Newspapers across the country advertised the lottery, and a lucky winner might walk away with a sensational prize like Hiram Powers's *Greek Slave*, a near lifesize marble nude valued, even then, in the thousands of dollars. Losers received an engraving worth near the subscription price, so everyone was happy. G. B. Warren, organizer of an 1860–61 YMA exhibition, wrote to the painter John Kensett to explain: "A few gentlemen have clubbed together here with a view of securing some pictures for our next Winter's Exhibition and for distribution in this city, each subscribing $100 and after the Exhibition to distribute by lot the pictures among the subscribers – no profit to anyone except to the artists and the person drawing a picture to pay for the frame." (The Troy gentlemen who did not draw one of the pictures received no consolation prize other than the knowledge that they had contributed to the glory of their city through this display of wealth and culture.)

Warren, a Troy iron manufacturer and bank president, ordered a $250 picture "of any subject" from Kensett for the lottery and then went on to ask a favor: "I should like you to paint me a small sketch on paper in oils about 3 × 5 inches for a sketchbook I'm making up and be sure to put your initials to it, only I would like a nicely finished picture and not a scratch only. I have some English sketches of men of Eminence and I propose to get half a dozen by the finest American artists. . . ."[11]

Warren's request, which turns the sought-after sketch into a kind of celebrity autograph, hints at just how "art-mad" people were at this time and place. Between the 1840s and the 1860s, American cities devoured art – especially painting, and particularly, landscape painting – at a rate that astonishes today. (Between 1839 and 1851 the free gallery of the New York Art Union claimed an average yearly attendance of 250,000 persons, a number that equals 57 percent of the total population of New York City at that time. According to the *Knickerbocker Magazine* of 1848, this truly popular crowd included "noisy boys and girls" and "working men . . . by the hundreds.")

In Troy, a public feast of "ornamental" painting enlivened the whole city. The photographer William Henry Jackson painted window screens in the city as a boy in the mid- to late 1850s. He wrote in his autobiography: "At that time (and for many years afterward) window screens were more than mere utilitarian barriers to houseflies and mosquitoes. They were the medium for displaying some of the most astonishing pictorial art. . . . As you walked along Fourth Street on a summer's day . . . here were Mr. Jones' parlor windows parading the virtues of home life among the Romans; there were Mrs. Smith's testifying to her travels through the Black Forest and an idyllic honeymoon on Lake Lucerne; just beyond Dr. Robinson's eloquently spoke his love of grazing cows, old mills and waterfalls. It was a wonderful world. . . ."

The Gilbert Car Company carriage painters rated as the elite of the Troy decorative painters. A passenger on the Troy-Saratoga Railroad line c. 1840 left this description of the work:

> The outside of the cars is painted of a beautiful fawn colour, with buff shading, painted in "picture panels" with rose, pink, and gold borders, and deep lake shading; the small mouldings of delicate stripes of vermilion and opaque black. Within the panels are "transferred" some of the most splendid productions of the ancient and modern masters, among which are copies from "Leonardo da Vinci," "Horace Vernet," "David," (the celebrated painter to Napoleon) "Stuart," and many more of the modern school. The whole number of the subjects of the twenty-four cars cannot fall far short of two hundred, as each car averages from six to ten subjects.[12]

In mid-July 1855, a correspondent of the *Troy Daily Times* visited the then new Gilbert plant on Green Island. He viewed several new omnibus bodies with picture panels on them. There were action scenes: a French artilleryman in the Crimea (he had evidently received a fresh gunshot wound, as his head is bandaged), and a wreck at sea, showing the dismemberment of the vessel, and passengers clinging to shattered spars and broken hull. But the omnibuses also featured unpeopled landscapes and seascapes: "a mountain brook whose waters are bounding forward in little elfish cascades" and "a fishing smack at sea."

The world of the Troy ornamental painters did not survive long – at least not beyond the decade following the Civil War. Photography, cheap prints, manufactured wallpapers – all these things drove decorative painting of this kind from existence. As early as 1862, when Seneca Ray Stoddard came

to work at Gilbert's, the painting department may have already fallen from the height of its glory. (William Richardson Tyler claimed that the collapse of carriage-painting had forced him out on his own in 1858.) By Stoddard's day, exterior picture panels had disappeared from omnibus bodies and railway cars. Stoddard painted landscape scenes on the interiors of cars.

Stoddard's early working life followed the traditional timetable of a craftsman's progress. While no definite information on his apprenticeship years survives, he started work at the Gilbert plant at age nineteen – the age at which a young man usually left poorly paid or unpaid apprentice labor and went out as a journeyman (a by-the-journée [day] worker). With sufficient earnings and opportunity, the journeyman then established himself as a master craftsman in his own business at twenty-one – which is exactly what Stoddard did.

On August 23, 1864, just a few months after his twenty-first birthday, Stoddard advertised in the *Glens Falls Republican* as a "House, Sign, and Ornamental" painter. Seven months later, he joined forces with G. E. Norris, the son of a family of carriagemakers and blacksmiths. The two men rented the "Paint Shops of J. H. Norris on Ridge Street" and declared themselves ready "to do all kinds of Carriage, House, Sign, Banner, and Ornamental Painting in the best style and at reasonable prices."[13] The house painting advertised was interior, decorative work – probably wall murals and painted chimney backs.

Stoddard belongs to the very last generation of craft-trained artists. By the 1880s, the craft or otherwise modest origins of many distinguished painters already looked strange to people. A Frederick White wrote in the *Art Amateur* of March 1883: "One was a wheelright, another a carpenter, a third a carriage-painter, a fourth a bartender, a fifth a doctor's office lad, and the sixth an unsuccessful furrier's apprentice. . . . It is amazing that each one of that Albany group has made for himself a name. The art world knows them today as E. D. Palmer, the sculptor, James M. Hart, Lamon [sic] Thompson, Edward Gay, William Hart and George Boughton."

Painters associated with luminism – the art style that John Wilmerding finds in Stoddard's photography – often had strong roots in the older, more egalitarian, craft world. John Kensett (1816–1872) began his working life as an engraver. Fitz Hugh Lane (1804–1865) was briefly a shoemaker, but, more to the point, he functioned partly as an ornamental painter almost until the end of his life. He painted an elaborate shop sign for a Gloucester merchant in 1855. Martin Heade (1814–1904) received his first lessons in art from Edward Hicks, a Quaker neighbor in Bucks County, Pennsylvania, who made a living as a coach and sign painter, but is best known today as the creator of the remarkable series of *Peaceable Kingdom* paintings.

The career of another luminist, Sanford Gifford (1823–1880), follows a different pattern, one more like that of artists' lives in the future. Like Frederick Church, Gifford was the son of a wealthy man, and like Church, he received all his art training in the studios of other fine artists. Gifford studied with John Reuben Smith, Church with Thomas Cole. Gifford also attended Brown University before going to New York City to work under Smith.

But Gifford experienced the passing of the craft world in another way. His father owned the iron foundry in Hudson, New York, which in the space of a generation converted a pretty town into a grimy,

industrial city. According to Gifford's biographer, Ila Weiss, the factory "ultimately filled twelve acres of the bay with slag, cinders, and other waste, thereby contributing to the decline of the city."

It wasn't just painters and ironworkers whose training and opportunities changed across the middle of the century. This happened in a wide range of occupations, and it was a painful thing for many. Stoddard had two cousins who were printers in Glens Falls,[11] and their craft suffered an early devaluation of skills. A Stoddard contemporary, Samuel Clemens, who used the pseudonym Mark Twain (1835–1910), earned barely more than his board as a journeyman printer in New York City in the 1850s. One reason for this was the flood of Irish immigrants into the profession. Clemens's brother, Orion, a master printer, lived a life of increasing desperation and poverty in the 1850s and later. The new times (and Mark Twain wrote about some of them in his 1873 novel, *The Gilded Age*) disturbed many people profoundly and made best-sellers of two books that recalled the pre-industrial village through a golden haze of memory: Mark Twain's *The Adventures of Tom Sawyer* and Louisa May Alcott's *Little Women*. Both novels were written for adults about a childhood world that was truly lost. In the old world, Mark Twain's father, John Clemens, had simultaneously filled the occupations of judge, lawyer, and wagonmaker in one small Tennessee town. And Samuel Stoddard, Sr., had trained one son as a minister (Parley) and another as a shoemaker (John). Samuel Stoddard's grandson, Seneca, was trained to take his place in the craft world too, but already a huge wave of new technologies – which included photography – was churning up the familiar landscape.

Keene Valley east of Beede House

Blue Ridge, from Root's Hotel

The Adirondacks, a view at North Elba

This view from St. Regis Mountain is one of a series taken from the site for the New York State Survey of the Adirondacks.

Little Tupper Lake

(Opposite) Indian Head, Lower Au Sable Lake

45

Running the rapids at Saranac Lake. The canoeists had to hold their craft steady for this "action" shot.

A "Jam" at Luzerne Falls

(Above) A Good Story. An Adirondack lumber shanty

(Left) Mount Morris, from the Outlet at Tupper Lake

Camp on the Upper Au Sable Lake. Stoddard stands at the left: the camera shutter release cable can be seen extending from the base of the lean-to running across the forest floor.

An Adirondack house. This house, with its characteristic Adirondack camp roof of hemlock bark,
stood at Bassett's Carry on Utowana Lake, between Eagle Lake and Raquette Lake.

Alvah Dunning, a celebrated guide and Adirondack character

(Above) A young Indian woman at Lake George

(Left) Avalanche Pass

53

Game in the Adirondacks

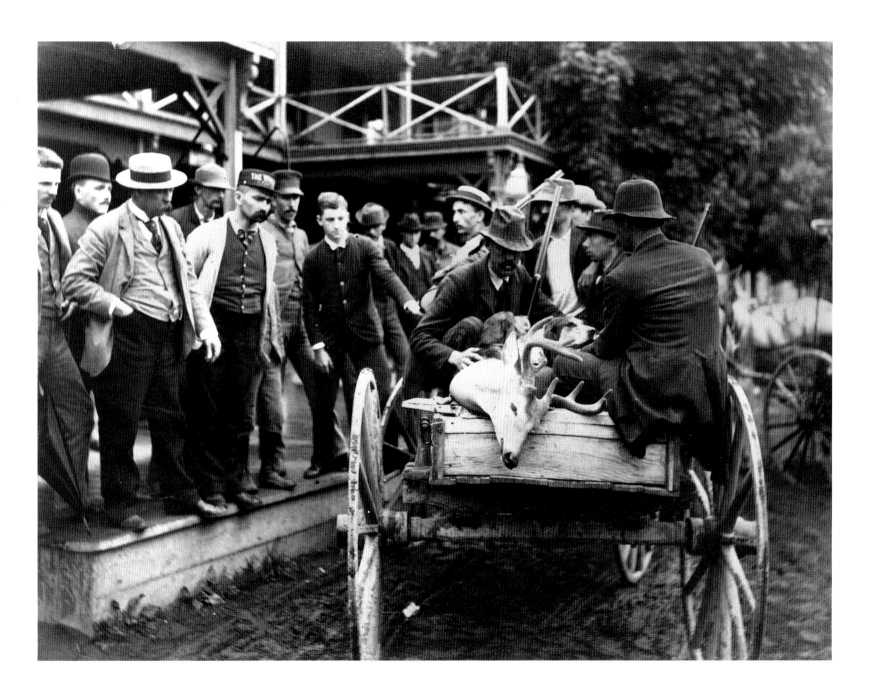

Hunters return to the Windsor Hotel at Elizabethtown, New York.

Stoddard is the man in the white hat in the lean-to.

Adirondack hunters

Hulett's Landing,
Lake George

Chapter Two
GLENS FALLS

The City of Glens Falls sits on the north bank of the Hudson River in Warren County, less than ten miles as the crow flies from Stoddard's birthplace in Wilton. It mushroomed into existence across the years of Stoddard's childhood and youth. Glens Falls had a population of more than 3,000 in 1860; by 1874, the combined populations of Glens Falls and South Glens Falls (the portion of the city located on the south bank of the river in Saratoga County) topped 10,000. During the 1860s, the city, technically still a village until 1908, supported an opera house, a music hall, eleven churches, and as many as three photographic galleries. Some of these studios had rather brief lives. One long-lived gallery (1862 through about 1890) was the establishment of George Conkey, who advertised "stereoscopic and other views made to order" all through the 1860s.[1] Other gallery advertisements of this time refer to portraits only.

From October 1866 through May of 1867, Conkey ran a regular advertisement in the *Glens Falls Messenger*, which declared in bold type: "Have You Seen the Banner?" and continued, "Those who have not are informed that by visiting Traphagan's Block, Ridge Street, They can see the Banner free of charge and by calling Up Stairs they will find Conkey in his New Gallery!"

Stoddard, who claimed to be a master in "Banner … painting" in his own advertisement of March 1865, may well have created this drawing card for Conkey's Gallery, and also worked there as a photographer and painter from the fall of 1866 through the spring of 1867. These dates fit nicely between Stoddard's "ornamental painting" notices of 1864–65, and, later, the first reference to his own independent photography in the fall of 1867.

Conkey (or another teacher) instructed Stoddard in the "wet-plate" photography of the day, which required an operator to work against the clock in a nerve-racking fashion. The photographer first coated one side of a 4" × 7" or 8" × 10" glass plate with a thick chemical called collodion, a recently (1847) invented substance with a bizarre origin. A military surgeon had discovered that pouring ether and alcohol on guncotton – the cotton wadding saturated with sulfuric and nitric acids that the Victorian Age used as cannon explosive – dissolved the guncotton into a jelly that dried into plastic-like sheets when spread thin. Doctors had employed collodion to seal up wounds, its only use until the photographic one.

Working quickly, the photographer did not let the collodion, which also contained an admixture of potassium iodide, dry on the glass plate. He had to dip the plate while still tacky in a five-minute bath of silver nitrate in the darkroom. This "excited" or sensitized the plate, which was then placed, wet, into the camera and exposed for a length of time varying from a fraction of a minute to several minutes. After exposure, the photographer hurried once again into the darkroom – for the wet plate must never dry out – washed it first in pyrogallic acid, then in "hypo," a solution of potassium cyanide, and finally in water. He next dried the negative over a candle flame and varnished it while still warm from the fire. The photographer then "printed" the image by placing a negative in contact with a photosensitized paper and passing a light through it. The paper was then developed in much the same way as the negative.

Stoddard and Conkey printed their images on papers that the manufacturer had already painted with a solution of albumen (egg white), potassium bromide, and acetic acid. Previously, photographers had to sensitize these papers themselves and dry them before use, Stoddard, Conkey, and their assistants printed by placing the papers beneath the glass negatives in full sunlight. The printer controlled results by the length of time he or she allowed the image to develop in the sunlight. But this was by no means the last step. Prints were washed, toned, fixed, and washed again. Toning subtly altered the color of prints; gold-toning, submersion in a gold-chloride solution, gave a red-brown cast to a picture.

The stereograph images that Conkey advertised, and that both Stoddard and Conkey produced in the 1860s and 1870s, were pairs of small pictures taken by a single camera with two small lenses fixed 2½" apart, about the distance that separates human eyes. The camera simultaneously exposed the almost identical images, side by side, on a 4" × 7" plate. After printing, the paired images, cropped into arch shapes on top, were glued onto a single card. A viewer could then gaze at the stereo card through a hand-held stereoscope for a three-dimensional effect.

If Stoddard trained or worked with Conkey, he did not make much of the episode. An account of his career in the *History of Warren County* (1885) reads:

From the time of his advent to Glens Falls [Stoddard] followed the business of sign and ornamental painting, giving his spare hours to landscape and portrait work. He learned the art of photography, with a view of thus securing by his own use of the camera broader opportunities to study the beautiful in nature, his artistic genius turning naturally more to landscape than to portrait work. As his collection of photographic negatives increased, embracing many of the grandest scenes in the Adirondack region and about Lakes George and Champlain, the prints began to be called for by tourists and others and Mr. Stoddard finally gave up shop work and devoted himself entirely to landscape photography, landscape and portrait painting, and latterly to the publication of books and maps.

(This passage must be close to Stoddard's own view of things because his friend and neighbor, A. W. Holden, wrote most of the Glens Falls material in the history.)

The earliest reference to Stoddard's photography appears in the October 1, 1867, edition of the *Glens Falls Republican*:

Mr. Stoddard, Photographer, has taken a number of instantaneous stereoscopic views of natural objects in this vicinity and especially about our beautiful falls. . . .

He has also photographed our banks and churches and several private dwellings with a vivid correctness and clearness of detail given only by sun pictures. Mr. Stoddard has chosen his objects with the eye of an artist.

A single, dated, large-plate photograph survives from the following year, 1868. This is a group portrait of a club of young Glens Falls men who camped and fished on one of the Lake George islands during the 1860s and 1870s. The next dated Stoddard photograph of larger than stereo size is another group portrait of the same club in 1870 (5½" × 9¼").[2] Evidently, Stoddard made large-plate photographs on Lake George during these years. Unfortunately, he didn't date any of this work except the club pictures. (From early in his career, he numbered his images for marketing purposes. His *Adirondacks Illustrated* of 1874 already lists photograph numbers through the 600s. But he frequently updated his roster of photographs, discarding some images and renumbering others, so that his catalogue numbers don't provide clear indications of the dates or sequence of his photographs.)

Most Stoddard photographs measure close to 4" × 7" or 6½" × 8". Images that exist in the unusual, roughly 6" × 10"-sized prints, attached to very large cardboard mounts, probably belong to this early period. Another example is a view of Sloop Island (page 62); it measures 5½" × 9⅛" affixed to a cardboard mount measuring 9¼" × 12¾".[3] (The two pictures of the Glens Falls club, the Waltonian Society, are mounted on similar cards.) Stoddard continued to produce small (3" × 3¾") stereo images, too. The files of the Chapman Museum contain more than a dozen of these, all Lake George subjects, dated 1870.

In November 1870, Stoddard returned from a trip into the Adirondacks with "a series of excellent stereoscopic views of Indian Pass, Henderson Lake, Long Lake, the Raquette River and other notable places." A later newspaper notice of this same month refers to Stoddard's "new series of Stereoscopic views of

The Presbyterian Church at Glens Falls

Sloop Island in Lake George

some of the most picturesque points on the Hudson River, Luzerne Lake, and gems of the Adirondacks."[4]

Yet in this same year, Stoddard opened a painting school, and his own painting and drawing rated at least three separate newspaper notices. In May the art audience was alerted to "some most excellent paintings of Lake George executed by the talented young artist S. R. Stoddard" and "an excellent portrait of Stoddard, the Artist, executed by himself." In November he showed *Lost in the Woods*, "a very fine original painting . . . by our young artist, S. R. Stoddard. It represents a bare-headed boy crouched at the foot of a grand old tree, with the ground and foliage of the forest in variegated autumnal hues. . . ."[5]

Stoddard's 1870 trip through the Adirondacks was a painting tour as much as a photographic one; the Adirondack Museum possesses a landscape, *Schroon River*, dated October 1870 (one of only a few dated Stoddard paintings). Stoddard cites his occupation as "landscape painter" on the 1870 census. In addition, he accepted two important portrait commissions in 1872.[6]

It was probably not until 1873 that his interest in and success with photography began to overwhelm any ambitions he had as a painter. He identified himself as a "landscape photographer" in an 1874 Glens Falls directory and on the 1875 census.[7]

During these years, numbers of prominent artist-photographers established studios and worked in both mediums. Weston Naef and James Wood write concerning the midcentury photographer of the West, A. J. Russell:

Russell went beyond using the camera simply for making notes; he found the photograph esthetically satisfying . . . . He described Spectre Lake in the Uinta Mountains, Utah Territory, thus: "To say the sun reveals untold beauties is commonplace indeed. Words cannot express or describe it. But the truthful camera tells the tale and tells it well." He compared the actual scene to the glass plate he made of it in August 1869 and noted: "The picture developed finely, and, forgetting the color in the magnificent effect, a picture, clean [and] sharp, and a peculiar softness pervading the whole, reconciled me at once to the loss of color."

Without doubt, Stoddard, like Russell, took reward and pleasure from his camera work. But the role and status of the photographer worried him a little. In October 1873, he wrote a long digression within a newspaper account of his trip into the Adirondacks of this year:

The average photographer nowadays is neither fish nor fowl and don't know just exactly where he does belong. Among painters he is looked upon as a scavenger in the field of art, doing all the dirty work; the poodelish [sic] fop and genteel counter-jumper looks down on him as a mechanic; some set him down as a magician – a man of mystery, others as one possessing supernatural power, who has sold himself to the Evil One and through him works wonders, while the world in general considers him a lazy, good-for-nothing sort of fellow who objects to work on phisicological [sic] principles, and who, when he couldn't get a job at saloon-keeping, took to photographing as the next best thing, with an irresistible inclination to tail "artist" on his name as soon as he learns to spell the word – which may occasionally be true.

And:

The photographer brought us trouble. His traps made drivers swear and our carriage look like an emigrant wagon; mothers frightened their tender innocents with the information that the gipsies [sic] were coming; impudent little boys made disrespectful observations and hung around to get a peep at that great, big, black box; the horses even – knowing brutes – catching sight of it and evidently concluding that "us had a funeral," broke into a walk and wanted to stop at every graveyard on our course. It was too much; we loved the photographer, but we also wanted to travel as gentlemen, so we voted him dead and – figuratively – packed him away in his big, black box with the other articles that we did not need and . . . got into a light buggy, sandwiched a driver in between us and started for North Elba.

Under all the jokes, Stoddard shrinks from the label "mechanic" and lays claim to that of "gentleman." He had a better claim to this last title than another area photographer of the day named George Irish. Irish took Alfred Stieglitz's portrait in the summer of 1873, just months before Stoddard wrote his laments about the photographer's lot. Stieglitz remembered Irish ("a tintyper at Lake George") as a "decidedly cross-eyed" man who spent a good deal of time touching up the portraits of his subjects with "a fine camel's hair brush [dipped] into some rouge."[9] Irish lived in Glens Falls and had a studio there by 1874. He appears in the 1870 census as a "photographist" of no estate, living in a boardinghouse occupied by day laborers, among others.[10]

Stoddard's situation looks quite different. On coming to Glens Falls, he immediately entered respectable circles. The 1865 census finds him living in the family of a wealthy merchant and insurance agent, Thomas Potter. Stoddard married Augusta Potter, the family's youngest child, on May 3, 1868. Two years later, he owned a house and lot worth $3,000 and headed a household containing his wife and baby son, his eighteen-year-old sister, Julia, and a live-in servant girl.[11]

But the landscape painter turned landscape photographer – who sought "broader opportunities to study the beautiful in nature" – spent some time taking portrait photographs in a studio setting. Two self-portraits of a very young-looking Stoddard survive, stamped with the legend "S. R. Stoddard Photo" within an oval mark.[12] In an article of October 1873 in the *Glens Falls Republican*, he also described very convincingly the problems of a portrait photographer:

> *Solemnly that man of darkness and curious smells goes for that infant. There is no buoyancy in his step for he feels that he is fighting against fate, and it is only from a sense of duty that he can bring himself to the scratch; but at last the instrument is pointed, the last ribbon adjusted, the last pat given, then comes a moment of awful silence as the cloth is lifted; mother and aunties stand with expectancy on their faces and their mouths wide open, and the central figure of this admiring circle, startled by this sudden lull in the storm, attempts to investigate. The disgusted photograph-man drops the cloth and marches to his darkroom to swear, while the women laugh hysterically, make a rush and devour the darling then clamor for a look at the picture, and think it's so funny that it's got two noses and four eyes and express a willingness to keep trying all day if necessary to get a good one; all of which is very gratifying to the victim.*
>
> *Then he tries again and they all get around and say, "look at auntie" and "ain't he nice" and "now's your time" and other like encouraging observations, just at the wrong time, and he keeps trying that baby until his patience is exhausted, and still he smiles a sickly smile as he disappears in the dark room to make some remarks to himself and gain strength for another trial. Suffering as only a photographer can suffer, who knows that this is a test case which will forever decide his future business relations with that family.*

Nineteenth-century artists often viewed portraiture, whether painted or photographic, as pedestrian business. It put bread on the table, but could not help them achieve the creative distinction of landscape, genre, or history scenes. That Stoddard turned away from portrait photography so early in his career is a clear mark of his ambition.

The Mariners. *A Lake George scene*

Lake George, in the Narrows

Lake George

Waiting at the dock at Roger's Rock Hotel, Lake George

On the beach, moonlight effect, Lake George

Crosbyside dock, Lake George, August 28, 1877. The Crosbyside was a large hotel.

Crosbyside Dock

Sheldon Point, Lake George

At Lake George

Horicon Sketching Club at Lake George

Hulett's Landing, Lake George

Horicon Pavilion, Lake George

Caldwell (today's Lake George Village) from Fort William Henry Hotel

The largest and grandest of the Lake George hotels was the Fort William Henry Hotel.

Homeward Bound. *At the Fort William Henry Hotel, Lake George*

*Blue Mountain
Lake House*

Chapter Three
PERSONA

Stoddard claimed an "elementary education" only, but he evidently educated himself with wide reading. And he reveals his breadth of literary acquaintance when he begins to write for publication. His earliest article for the *Glens Falls Messenger*, "From the Adirondacks – Scratchings by the Roadside" (1870), contains lines of poetry from William Cullen Bryant and Alexander Pope, as well as references to Poe, Gulliver, Münchhausen, and Virgil.

Stoddard wrote poetry himself – humorous pastiches of Longfellow or Poe, such as this section of a long poem of about 1872, written to advertise a musical evening at the photographer's Masonic lodge:

> *Members of the lodge called "Senate"*
> *With the hope of seeing ducats,*
> *With the blissful thoughts of greenbacks*
> *Falling like the leaves of autumn*
> *Down into their empty coffers,*
> *Meet each other now in secret,*
> *Practice many things in secret,*
> *That will shortly be made public.*
> *   And this is the explanation*
> *Of the sights and sounds mysterious,*
> *Of the pictures and the posters,*

Of the many colored hand-bills
 And the curious little dodgers
 That are scattered through the country.
     Pilgrim, pause and think it over;
 Go down deep into your pockets;
 Skirmish round among the buttons
 And the unpaid bills that stuff it;
 There perhaps among the rubbish,
 You may find an odd half-dollar;
 Or if you are unsuccessful
 Do not give it up in sorrow,
 But go straightway forth and borrow.
 Go without your Sunday dinner;
 Pawn your boots, your umbrella,
 Anything, but do not falter . . .

He wrote for the Glens Falls and Troy papers between 1870 and 1876, not just accounts of his trips into the Adirondacks but other kinds of reporting and commentary as well. He covered meetings of the temperance movement, the quasi-religious, quasi-political league that opposed any and all consumption of alcohol. He produced at least one highly colored temperance short story, "Rescued from Myself," which, interestingly, begins with a vision of sky and horizon: "I can see that day. White cumuli were heaped over the wood tops, but the middle sky was blue and clear. Though I was dozing on a saloon step, this day of beauty got through even my wavering sight...."[1] Stoddard also produced short comic pieces for the newspapers that were built around a fictional "old yankee" character, Hiram Green, or were based on real happenings in his Elm Street household. Compared to the Elm Street incidents,

the Mr. Green stories labor along lifelessly. Stoddard may even have worked as a staff writer for one Glens Falls paper, the *Glens Falls Republican*, in 1872–73.[2]

Twain's influence almost shouts from Stoddard's comic writing. It is no surprise to find a Twain newspaper piece glued into a scrapbook of Stoddard's own newspaper clippings. In a conscious or unconscious borrowing, Stoddard titled his first guidebook *Lake George: A Book of Today* (1873); Twain's novel of the same year, *The Gilded Age*, has the subtitle, "A Tale of Today." In 1873 and 1874, he brought out his first guidebooks to Lake George and the Adirondacks. These contain information on hotels and coach and railway routes as well as Stoddard's commentaries on local history and his own comic misadventures as a traveler. *The Adirondacks Illustrated*, his most popular guidebook, drew most of its text from Stoddard's newspaper accounts of his 1873 trip into the mountains. The books found an immediate market with the new wave of tourists to the region. Stoddard sold them by mail and through most of the Lake George and Adirondack hotels, as well as through bookstores in the major cities of the Northeast. He essentially reprinted the texts of these books in yearly editions through 1893, with small amounts of updated information.

Stoddard's writing output surged again in later life, in the 1890s and the first years of this century. He produced a book-length manuscript account of an 1883–86 canoe trip, *The Story of Atlantis* (1890); a 348-page travel book, *The Cruise of the Friesland* (1895); a 220-page novel in manuscript, *Jan the Golden* (1902); two novella-length stories, "Marsa Phil" and "Lex Talionis"; as well as issues of

Stoddard's Northern Monthly (later *Stoddard's Adirondack Monthly*) of 1906–08, which feature essays and stories on Adirondack subjects.

These writings tell a great deal about Stoddard's thoughts and hopes and other parts of his nature. The novels and articles from the turn of the century repeat the themes of the early articles and guide texts, sometimes even using the same words and metaphors. Among other things, Stoddard's writings reveal him as extremely sensitive to visual and other impressions, religious, highly sexed, politically conservative, and also someone who may have struggled with depression. Some of these qualities – the sensitive, spiritual, and perhaps psychologically tender parts of Stoddard's personality – link him in an interesting way with the luminist painters. Sanford Gifford, for example, was a "particularly sensitive person" whose older brother committed suicide in his twenties.[3] Contemporaries viewed Martin Heade as a withdrawn and moody person, and polio, or something like it, had crippled Fitz Hugh Lane as a child – thereby forcing on the painter a degree of both physical and psychological isolation. It is also true that the one robust extrovert among the group, John Kensett, produced most of his luminist works in the last years of his life. He actually painted a large proportion of his luminist landscapes in the summer of 1872, only months before his sudden death in his New York studio in December of that year.

The evidence for Stoddard's depression is not confirmed, but many things point toward it. Oddly enough, the relentlessly comic style of most of the early writing is one clue: pain often takes refuge in comedy. The sad events in Stoddard's life are not hard to find. His mother's death in 1851, when he was eight years old, dealt a hard blow. Other deaths clustered near hers: those of his grandmother, Leah Ray; his aunt, Miriam Ray; and also that of his infant sister, born in May 1851 and dead by September 1851. His father's speedy marriage to an eighteen-year-old girl, Laura Cook (she produced her first child in 1852), and the move from Dimick Corners in 1854, demanded further adjustments from Seneca Ray and his brothers.

Modern psychological theory points to just these circumstances – a number of deaths in the family, early remarriage of the surviving parent, and a major family move – as factors that tend to interrupt a child's mourning process for a lost parent and leave the child vulnerable to depression in later life. A study of the lives of two famous Americans, Abraham Lincoln and Meriwether Lewis, traces their severe depressions to one or more of these causes (multiple deaths for Lincoln; early remarriage and family relocation for Lewis).[4] Stoddard encountered all three negative factors.

It is interesting that Lincoln experienced much of his depression as self-described "hypochondriachal fits." Stoddard had an unusual concern about health, too, possibly aggravated by his brother Edward's illness and death in the 1870s. Edward named his eldest son, born in 1865, Seneca – one proof of a close relationship between the brothers. A photograph of Edward (in a composite of family photographs put together by Stoddard about 1876) shows an emaciated, almost skeletal man.[5]

The 1876 edition of *Lake George: A Book of Today* includes a lengthy (a full page and a half) discourse on the care and feeding of healthy children by one hotel proprietor. This is mostly an elaboration of the nugget: "Give 'em lots of exercise, and lots of pork too if they want it, and they'll never die with the consumption. . . ."

In his unpublished novel, *Jan the Golden*, Stoddard wrote about warriors and maidens of the Viking Age in Scandinavia. Yet a number of the characters are felled at different times by Camille-like wasting diseases. In one strange episode, the hero, Jan, no longer wishes to live because he has (temporarily) lost the heroine, Thyri. He allows his blood to be drained away and pumped into a dying British princess. The princess plays no part in the novel beyond this walk-on as the victim of a mysterious decline.

Some of his 1902 preoccupation with failing health may relate to Augusta Stoddard's illness with chronic gastroenteritis; she died in 1906.[6] But the classic wasting disease of the nineteenth century was tuberculosis, the disease that almost certainly killed Edward Stoddard.

All this raises the interesting possibility that Stoddard's art sprang partly from a search for his own health, that the trips into the wilderness to photograph and to paint were also attempts to strengthen himself and ward off tuberculosis. As early as the 1850s, nineteenth-century medicine advised consumptives, and those with consumptive tendencies, to take in as much fresh, cold air as possible.[7] In the late 1860s and early 1870s, Stoddard slept out regularly on Lake George aboard an open sailboat. He traveled into the mountains frequently over the next decade, remaining in the Adirondacks between July and December of 1878 with a New York State survey team. He apparently made a month-long canoe trip in 1881 as well as the extended one of 1883–86 – the so-called *Atlantis* trip – which took him in stages down the Hudson River and then north around the New England coast to the Bay of Fundy in Canada.

Another reading of Stoddard's journeys also relates to depression. Meriwether Lewis benefited from and craved the violent exertions of his famous expedition because strenuous physical activity relieved his depressions. The dangers of the venture also attracted the suicidal Lewis, who eventually shot himself. Stoddard's work for the New York State Survey of the Adirondacks in 1878 rates as strenuous. This project called for the scientific mapping of the extremely rugged Adirondack region, until this time only a crudely guessed-at and sketched-in portion of all charts. The leader of the expedition, Verplanck Colvin, called it "a season of constant, severe, and most intense work," during which Stoddard and assistants climbed "Whiteface Mountain, St. Regis Mountain, the Camel's Hump on Noon Mark Mountain, Raven Hill, etc. etc." and took "more than 200 . . . special photographs . . . complete circles of the horizon."[8]

The 1883–86 canoe trip in the *Atlantis* was dangerous as well as physically demanding. The venture inspired a controversy within the American Canoe Association. Stoddard and his companion, a young man named Roswell B. Burchard, were ACA members. The association magazine, *The American Canoeist*, condemned the voyage in an editorial of September 1883: "The route laid out by Mr. Stoddard was over waters where it is next to foolhardy to ven-

ture in a small boat . . . a canoe is not built or intend-
ed for such cruising as one gets even in Long Island
Sound." Stoddard pushed on with the trip even after
near-shipwreck ended the first leg of the journey.
Stoddard did not destroy himself like Meriwether
Lewis. He lived on into old age and worked until the
last five years of his life. Yet the fact of the perilous
voyage is there to wonder about.

The photographer's acutely sensitive nature
shows up throughout his writings in imagery in
which the natural landscape appears to shift or move:

> *. . . glittering sand that seemed to tremble in ecstasy
> under the heat waves of an unclouded sun. . . .*[9]

> *To the south lay the great peaks of the Adirondacks
> . . . a long line of giants, their dark blue crests rising
> like ocean billows . . . away toward the west a lower
> set of mountain waves are seen. . . .*[10]

> *The rolling sides of the mountains, beyond the
> ravine, seemed like huge waves and a feeble breeze
> that exposed the silvery sides of the leaves gave a
> touch to the whole that resembled breaking spray.
> The mountains beyond were as other waves. . . .*[11]

This way of seeing – where stationary objects
turn fluid – resembles that of ecstatic religious experience. Clearly Stoddard had a religious nature,
although this found expression in him mainly outside any formal church. Raised a Methodist, he may
have joined the Baptist Church on his marriage to
Augusta Potter (they were married by the Baptist
minister of Glens Falls). But by the end of his life he

An Adirondack Survey camp near Long Lake

Stoddard photographed himself in a sail canoe, probably on the Richelieu River.
He titled the print A Toiler of the Sea.

rejected both these denominations. At the time of his death in 1917 he made it clear that "He wanted no minister [at his funeral]. . . ."[12] Augusta Stoddard also turned away from the traditional churches and embraced Christian Science at some time in mid-life.

Like Ralph Waldo Emerson, Stoddard looked for God in unspoiled nature. He alludes to such a belief early on; his 1874 guidebook, *Adirondacks Illustrated*, contains this passage: "'Who would hesitate for one moment between the dusty city and a life among the grand old forests and lakes?' said the schoolmaster. 'How beautiful this free temple where every thought is an anthem of praise and thanksgiving.'" Stoddard also wrote a story for the *Northern Monthly* magazine called "The Phantom Bell" (July 1908) in which the hero, a New York clubman who comes to the Adirondacks for his health, expresses the same ideas more fully:

> *My ramblings into the holy of holiest of Natures temples, through the colonnades of the stately giants of the forest and under the blue vault of heaven, invigorated my jaded body and was healing my mind that had been poisoned by the wines of folly of civilization. Here I found my true self. Here I heard the first whispering of a smothered conscience. Here I was imbibing the first principles of primitive worship. Here I felt the connecting link that holds in unity a creation and its creator. . . . What right has man to destroy such a scene as this by making it a habitation? No more than he has a right to pre-empt the choice sites on the celestial river and thereby crowd the angels to planets new where civilization has not yet corroded the realm.*

Stoddard also looked for God in a new and different kind of religious belief: spiritualism. The American spiritualist movement arose out of a series of strange events that occurred in a farmhouse west of Rochester, New York, in 1848. Two teenage sisters, Margaretta and Katie Fox, began to report messages in the form of rappings and knockings from a man who was reputed to have been murdered in the farmhouse several years before. The sisters soon took to the lecture circuit and attracted a huge following and many imitators. Horace Greeley, the influential "radical Republican" editor of the *New York Tribune*, supported the claims of the Fox sisters.

Sanford Gifford, whose painting either directly or indirectly influenced Stoddard's photography, also had contacts with spiritualism.[13] (The Troy area was rather a hotbed of the activity. According to Whitney Cross, the investigator of enthusiastic religion in New York: "the industrial town of Troy was warm [for spiritualism and revivalistic religion] and the commercial town of Albany cold.") In Glens Falls, a homeopathic physician, George Little, organized a spiritualist society. A brother of his, Meredith Little, wrote a pamphlet on the subject.[14]

In the 1860s and 1870s, interest in spiritualism often formed part of an intellectual package that included liberal politics (meaning abolitionist, pro-black sentiments), support for the temperance movement and for homeopathic medicine. The opposition cluster of beliefs was conservative politics (non-radical Republicans or Democrats with markedly anti-black views) and a disposition in favor of traditional drink, medicine, and religion. Two Glens Falls newspapers, the *Glens Falls Messenger* (liberal) and the *Glens Falls Republican* (conservative), vigorously asserted the two different outlooks through the 1860s and early 1870s. Their voices moderated in later years as the issues themselves faded a bit.

Stoddard belonged to the same Masonic lodge as Meredith Little, and he painted a large mural of ghosts and spirit figures for the lodge. He also made a clear statement of his spiritualist interests in some of his photographs from the 1890s, painting ghosts and sprites onto the negatives of some of these. In one, little creatures dance above the head of an old Indian woman crouched by a fire. In others, trolls and goblins surround Scandinavian subjects.[15]

Stoddard's early writings hint at spiritualist sympathies as well. His account of an ascent of Whiteface Mountain in the 1874 *Adirondacks Illustrated* tells of following a trail of dainty, feminine footprints up the mountain path to the summit, where they abruptly vanished: "the feeling took possession of us that our 'Little Footprints' had taken wings and flown up among the angels, just a little higher than where we stood." A paragraph beyond the description of this slightly otherworldly experience comes the phrase: "a mantle of tender blue haze, seen only in autumn – not smoke – but something that suggests the thought of the myriad millions of pale sweet ghosts of falling leaves and dying flowers."

An early Stoddard newspaper piece suggests one attraction of spiritualism for the photographer and others of his age when many people died prematurely. The passage, which describes a temperance meeting in a Weaverton schoolhouse, is worth reading for its tone as well. It is visionlike in its intensity:

The bright sunshine was over all, shining warmly on the open spots from which the snow had melted on the great ragged-edged, cat-topped rocks out in front, making the house roofs glisten, the rippling water to sparkle like diamonds and pouring a flood of gold in through the open windows and door and across the floor, now spotlessly clean and worn by the feet of children for nearly 40 years until the knots stand up above the softer grain like the sharp-pointed hills and mountain peaks above the narrow valleys below; and to us in warm waves from the south, came the breath of spring, just awakened and bearing with it the crisp, invigorating freshness caught from the snowdrifts as it came over the mountains and down the hillsides to where we waited. What a flood of old time recollections came with that morning service, suggesting another schoolroom with its bright happy faces of boys and girls, some of them now grown to men and women, some peacefully sleeping under the quickening sod, and some cheated of that blessing, lost in the bloated diseased form [from] which rum has driven the old remembered spirit. . . .[16]

Between 1872 and 1877, Glens Falls newspapers recorded Stoddard's regular presence at temperance meetings. He took a leading role in the movement, serving as Warren County District Officer of the Sons of Temperance in 1872, and Grand Worthy Patriarch of the Eastern Division of the society in 1875. He assumed this last office at a convention held in New York City; the Eastern Division included Long Island and all the eastern part of the state.[17]

On the issues of spiritualism and temperance, Stoddard fits the profile of an idealistic, self-improving

Glens Falls Messenger reader. Stoddard also enjoyed a friendship with Dr. Austin Holden, president of the Warren County Homeopathic Society. Holden lived near Stoddard on Elm Street in Glens Falls, and he provided Stoddard with some of the local history background for his first guidebook, *Lake George.*

But from 1872, Stoddard wrote frequently for the conservative *Glens Falls Republican.* An editor of the *Messenger* attacked him personally in 1873 as "The Ray-less Satellite who muddles the 'religious' ragbag of the Democratic organ of this village. . . ."[18] (The "religious ragbag" must refer to Stoddard's coverage of temperance meetings.)

Stoddard's views on race reveal an intolerance that was borne out in other ways. His 1874 guidebook account of a visit to John Brown's grave in North Elba reveals little sympathy for the cause of black Americans. He comments negatively on the abolitionist hero Brown, "whose presence was marked by dissensions and bloodshed; who urged men on to murder in the name of freedom and read his bible all the time. . . . A fanatic he undoubtedly was." In Stoddard's words, Brown's actions "tended to precipitate the war by which, through rivers of blood, four million slaves went free." This last statement expresses little enthusiasm for the positive achievements of the war, and his late short story, "Marsa Phil," makes this point again. The narrator of "Marsa Phil," an ex-slave, regrets the carefree days of slavery and talks with approval about his ex-master's attacks on carpetbaggers and oppressive Union soldiers.

The account of the North Elba trip to John Brown's grave includes the portrait of a black driver named "Att" who takes Stoddard to the gravesite and delivers this epitaph for Brown's failed colony of freed slaves: "they couldn't make a livin' heah, too cold for 'em; wa'nt much used to work, I guess, an' couldn't stan' the kind they got heah. Most of 'em was barbers an' sich, who thought they wouldn't have nothin' to do when they came heah, an after the ol' man died they couldn't get along. . . ."

Stoddard describes "Att" as "a good-looking fellow, intelligent, well-informed, and decidedly attractive in his way, even if his skin *was* a few shades darker than regulation and his hair unexplorable in its kinkiness." Natural human sympathy struggles with a conviction that dark skin and "kinked" hair place "Att" in an alien category, outside normal concern. This attitude echoes in the photographer's negative portrayals of Irish immigrants in newspaper pieces of the 1870s as well as in passing slights cast at Italian immigrants and Jews in the pages of the *Northern Monthly.*

Curiously, while many nineteenth-century temperance advocates supported the rights of African Americans with devotion and energy, they tended to take a dim view of the mostly Catholic immigrants just arrived or arriving in this country. A description of the membership of the turn-of-the-century Anti- Saloon League, a late manifestation of the temperance movement, almost draws a picture of Stoddard's circumstances:

Methodism, North and South, gave the league its unanimous institutional support and supplied most of its militant leadership. The Baptists and Presbyterians, North and South, were not far behind. . . . Every major historian of the campaign, moreover, emphasizes other, non-theological factors that identify this form of Protestantism more exactly. Most obviously it was rural or small town; and its ancestry was British. Its deepest antipathies were directed toward city dwellers, foreigners, and Roman Catholics. Bigotry and nativism were often dry.

In an article of 1870, Stoddard draws an unflattering sketch of a character named Pat, "a young 'furriner.'" Pat tries to ride the Lake George stagecoach without a ticket while protesting himself innocent of such a "mane thrick." Stoddard also points to the Irishman as a stereotypical whiskey drinker and purveyor of whiskey. In the temperance story "Rescued from Myself": "A good-natured Patrick came slyly with a bottle and bade me [the recovering drunkard] 'whist at it.'"

Stoddard's comments on a Game License Law of 1908 reveal his contempt for both poor immigrant laborers and the powerful industry (the railroad) that employed them. At the same time, he shows tenderness and regard for native farm families:

> *the income of these hirelings of a vicious monopoly will not admit of their taking out twenty-dollar licenses very generally. No license, no hunt! Even a dago should be able to grasp this fact. . . . A twenty-dollar license fee by hunters who come from outside the State for the sport furnished by the Adirondacks is right enough. Also the payment of the small fee of $1.00 by city visitors or those who come from other counties is little enough, but . . . to most of the families who spend their lives in the wilderness, where the boys are expert hunters at ten, a dollar is not to*

be thrown away in the purchase of what they have always considered their inalienable right.

The narrator of "Marsa Phil" makes a comment that also reflects Stoddard's anti-city, anti-immigrant bias. The old slave remembers the opening days of the war: "Some – specially de tradin' people an de folks in de city – come out foh de Nof, while de ol' famblys [who provide the hero and heroine of the story] was genally strong foh de Souf."

Stoddard's contemporary, Mark Twain, took a larger and warmer view of humanity. He donated money to establish scholarship funds for black students and wrote and spoke against anti-Semitism. (Stoddard alludes to the anti-Jewish "restrictions" of one Adirondack hotel as a passing joke only.[19]) Twain's biographers point to childhood bonds with several motherly black women as a source of his later open and generous opinions. For whatever reasons, Stoddard did not develop such a generous outlook.

Stoddard's nativism shows a positive face in his admiration for Will Carleton, a now nearly forgotten poet who wrote about village and country life (*Farm Ballads*, 1873, and *Farm Festivals*, c. 1880). Stoddard quoted Carleton and clipped at least one of his poems from the newspaper. There was definitely nothing alien about Carleton (1845–1912), who was a Methodist from Michigan, the state where many of Stoddard's own family had settled by the 1870s. By the turn of the century, Carleton lived in Brooklyn, New York, and published a magazine called *Will Carleton's Everywhere* (1894–1913). This enterprise may have inspired Stoddard's own magazine *Northern Monthly* (1906–08).

The steamer Killoquah *at Raquette Lake*

Killoquah, *seen at the foot of Raquette Lake*

(Above) Stevens House, Lake Placid

(Right) Mirror Lake House, Lake Placid

Blue Mountain Tramps

Martin's Hotel, Saranac Lake

Slide, from Roger's Rock Hotel

Glass Globe at Fort William Henry Hotel, Lake George

Camp life at Lake George, August 7, 1876

(Above) Patients from the Trudeau Sanitorium take the air in a lean-to.

Lake House lawn; Beadleston Cottage

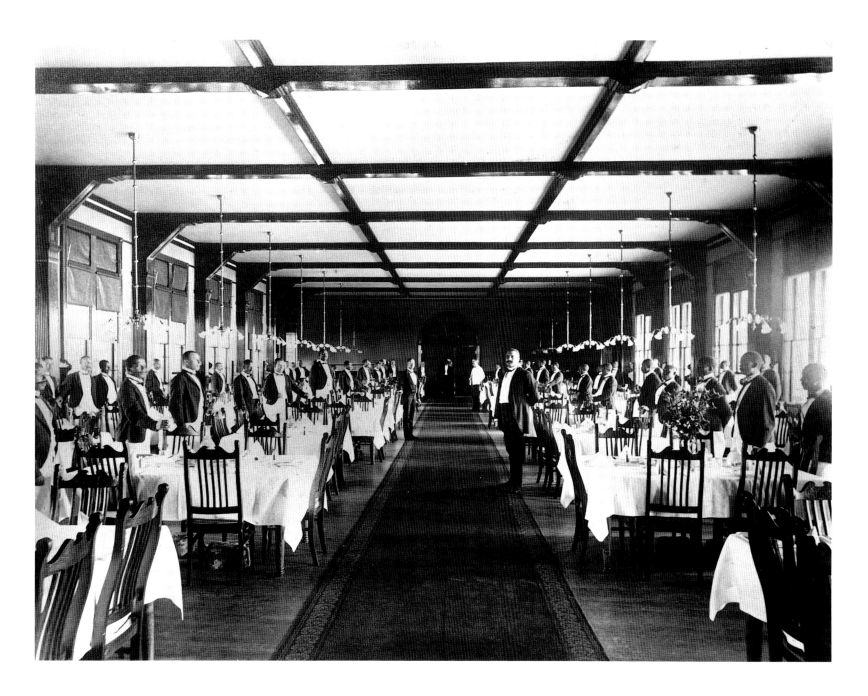

Hotel Champlain dining room

Prospect House verandah, Blue Mountain Lake

Fort William Henry Hotel "piazza," from the west

The interest in Carleton's poetry connects with the theme of a handful of Stoddard photographs, in which a boy sits alone in a rural or wilderness setting. These differ from the large number of photographs in which he pictured single adults surveying a wilderness scene. In these, a foreground figure is viewed from behind or occasionally from the side as he, or sometimes she, gazes out at a panorama. Stoddard placed the boys at or near the mid-distance of the photographs, facing toward the camera.

Stoddard links childhood with the rural or wilderness world in these images. He surely drew on his feelings about his early home towns, Wilton and Burke, in making them. His reference to boys who were "expert hunters at ten" calls up a picture of a Stoddard childhood spent hunting, fishing, and perhaps canoeing along the fringes of the Adirondack wilderness.

For companions in Wilton and Burke, Stoddard had his brothers, Edward and Charles. In adulthood, Stoddard traveled and worked with a series of brother-like companions. His first assistants were, in fact, his brothers: Charles Oblenis, who became his brother-in-law in the mid-1870s, and Frank Stoddard, Laura Cook's son and Seneca Ray Stoddard's half brother. Oblenis worked for Stoddard from at least 1873 through 1879, during which time he and Julia Stoddard Oblenis lived in his employer's household. Oblenis was a photographer "who did much of S. R.'s developing," according to the memory of one Stoddard family descendant. Oblenis made the first leg of the voyage of the *Atlantis*, the long canoe trip of 1883, with Stoddard. At some point in the 1880s, he and his wife moved to Michigan.

Frank (1852–1943) worked for his half brother

from the early 1870s, too, although never on a full-time basis. He listed his occupation as "lineman" (evidently for the local power company) on the 1880 census, and by the 1890s held the position of foreman or night engineer at the Glens Falls power station. In a 1962 interview with Maitland De Sormo, Frank's grandson remembered that Frank was short but very rugged. He had the reputation of being a very hard worker as a lumberman, and he did much of the heavy packing and rowing for Seneca. He also helped with the construction of Stoddard's studio atop the house at 22 Elm Street.

During the 1890s, a young photographer from Ballston Spa (just southeast of Saratoga Springs, New York) worked as Stoddard's assistant. This photographer, Jesse Wooley, accompanied Stoddard on trips in the Adirondacks, to the 1893 World's Fair in Chicago, to California and the Southwest, and into nearby Vermont. Wooley, originally from the town of Wilton, told the story of his service to and collaboration with Stoddard in a now-vanished diary.[20]

In the 1880s and 1890s, Stoddard also traveled with two wealthy New York clubmen, Wallace Bruce and Roswell B. Burchard, who were rather like the ones he wrote about in "The Phantom Bell." They were, of course, neither employees of Stoddard's nor photographic assistants, but on some expeditions they took the places of men who were.

Wallace Bruce was a literary gentleman, a friend of artists and writers in New York City. Just a year older than Stoddard, he produced books of poetry at about two-year intervals between 1878 and 1907. He owned a house in Poughkeepsie, and much of his poetry focused on the Hudson River and surrounding landscape. (Bruce's books include *The Hudson*, 1882, *From the Hudson to the Yosemite*, 1889, and *The Hudson Panorama*, 1888.) Bruce hired the artist James Smillie, who had a family house in Poughkeepsie, to illustrate two of his books.

Smillie and his brother George painted in Keene Valley in the Adirondacks at different times during the last decades of the century. It may be that it was through the Smillie brothers that Stoddard met Wallace Bruce in Keene Valley, or perhaps on Lake George – one of the meeting places of the American Canoe Association. Bruce and Stoddard possibly took a canoe trip from Canada into the Adirondacks near Clear Lake in 1881 (if the "R. W. B." who describes the trip in the association magazine is indeed [Robert] Wallace Bruce, and his camera-carrying friend "S_____," Seneca Ray Stoddard).[21]

Toward the end of his life, Bruce owned a winter home in De Funiak Springs, Florida, where he organized an annual winter lecture series; he invited Stoddard to lecture there in 1900, 1901, and 1902. His hospitality probably had something to do with Stoddard's illustrated lecture on the American South, "The Land of Flowers," as well as the "Marsa Phil" story.

Roswell B. Burchard was the second New Yorker. Nearly twenty years younger than Stoddard, Burchard agreed to accompany the photographer on the rest of the *Atlantis* canoe voyage after Oblenis could not or would not continue. In 1892, Burchard made a two-month trip to Alaska with Stoddard. Like Bruce, this young man had some literary interests. His 1932 obituary states that he "formerly was a correspondent for *The New York Herald*, *The New York Mail and Express*, and *Forest and Stream*." Later

in life, he ventured into politics and served as Republican lieutenant governor of Rhode Island from 1912 to 1914.

Stoddard moved easily among the wealthy and educated, although he apparently did so alone. Evidently, his wife Augusta Potter, known as "Gussie," took little part in these contacts with literary and sporting gentlemen from outside Glens Falls. She remained at home with the couple's two children, Charles Herbert, born in 1869, and LeRoy, born in 1876. She may also have traveled little because of ill health. From perhaps as early as her thirties, Augusta suffered intermittent bouts of the gastroenteritis that eventually killed her in her fifties. (This kind of sickness was rather common in nineteenth-century America.)

Virtually none of Stoddard's personal letters survive, and his relationship with Augusta, therefore, is unknown. Judging from photographs, she was very beautiful as a young woman and thereafter alternated between a kind of gaunt, nervous state and a robust, matronly one – depending upon her health.

We know, however, from other writings of Stoddard's that he was a passionate man. During his youth, especially, he wrote passages of description heavily freighted with sexual imagery:

from the dripping mine, a thousand feet down under the mountain side, from where the heavy stampers crush the gathered ore and where the glowing rods like fiery serpents hiss and squirm along the blackened floor. . . .[22]

Once more they come from the furnace, glowing red and as the flat bars pass through the last set of rollers it comes forth nearly round. Now it is passed rapidly through, back and forth, each time lengthening out farther than before, and as it is constantly forced along, it writhes and squirms about on the black floor like a serpent of fire – a string of red hot iron seventy feet in length....[23]

There is even an erotic flavor to his 1906 word picture of the beginning of the world:

And glowing with fervent heat the earth began its endless round. As through the ages the seething mass grew cool, scoria formed and floated, covering over with a roughened crust as the icepack of the North shuts in the heaving waters, while the clouds of steam that in a far-reaching nimbus had enveloped all, condensing fell in sheeted rain....[24]

The erotic energy that surfaces in Stoddard's writing surely powered the photographs in some way too. Peter Gay and others have written on the sexual component in the tremendous outpourings of work that Victorian artists and scholars left behind them. Stoddard was a true Victorian in terms of achievement; he produced a mountain of work in the form of painting, photography, and writing. Without doubt, the new sexual controls of the nineteenth century (driven by ideas of the natural purity of women plus an increasing need to control births) made their impress on Stoddard's creative life. Augusta's uncertain health may have further restricted sexual expression within the couple's marriage.

Augusta Stoddard was also an artist. At least one sketch of hers survives, a pencil drawing of an elabo-

rate flower arrangement signed "Augusta Potter." Maitland De Sormo reproduced a photograph of Augusta as a mature woman in his biography of Stoddard. This shows her sitting against a tree with one hand a blur as she sketches in a notebook. She and another woman, Emily Doty, who became Stoddard's second wife, did much of Stoddard's printing work in his studio atop the Elm Street house. It is interesting to find this "hidden" woman's work in the production of Stoddard's photographs. Stoddard paid Doty and his half sister Julia for both studio and household chores throughout the 1870s.

During the same years that he painted, photographed, and wrote, Stoddard also pursued scientific and technical matters. This says as much about the time in which he lived as it does about Stoddard's personal interests. In an article dated September 28, 1873, he casts a scientist's eye on the geological record of the earth's crust:

Ausable River... dashing downward between the towering cliffs on either side – apparently at some time rent asunder by a grand convulsion of nature – and passing for nearly a mile through depths and over rocks.... There are but two or three places where the descent into the bottom's caves can be safely made, the walls being in most places perpendicular nearly two hundred feet in height, from twenty to a hundred feet apart, and broken here and there by lateral fissures where projections on the one side are faced by indentations on the other, corresponding exactly in form, and showing conclusively that at some time away back this shell of rocks has cracked and drawn apart as we sometimes see clay in the road, sun-dried after a summer's shower. The wonder with me is that this miniature Yosemite at our very doors is so little known.

Stoddard's scrutiny of the cliffs and boulders of the Adirondacks follows in the tradition of the great nineteenth-century geologists, Alexander von Humboldt and Louis Agassiz, who saw God's plan in the traces of long-ago upheavals and glaciers.

The pass seems to have been caused by some mighty power that turned neither to the right nor left, but striking this mountain range passed through and onward, carrying everything before it. . . .[25]

The introduction to Stoddard's 1892 lecture, "The Adirondacks Illustrated," or "The Pictured Adirondacks," confidently meshes the words of Genesis with a kind of reverse "Big Bang" theory:

'In the beginning God created the heaven and the earth. And the earth was waste and void.' Matter impalpable filled space illimitable as fogs float in the viewless air. 'And God said – Let there be light!' The Divine Word smote through chaos and brooding matter hastened to obey feeling that new, strange power that we call gravitation drawing the scattered atoms as he willed, with added motion gaining ever increasing energy. Swift and swifter from the boundaries of vast areas it plunged, through fields of space to alloted centres, and in that crushing impact fierce suns and blazing planets flashed out, 'And there was light!'

Under the law that gathers the mist into rain-drops; shapes the rounded hailstone in the higher air and forms molten metal hurled from ruptured furnace into perfect spheres – flaming suns that burn for untold ages; great planets and their lesser moons, quick frozen in the icy void, went wheeling in their appointed orbits under immutable laws that are because He willed it.[26]

In January 1874, Stoddard acted as the impresario for two science exhibitions at the Glens Falls Opera House. The first was a course of three lectures by Professor W. C. Richards on "'The Matter Queen' which is the history, exploits and powers of hydrogen," on electricity and magnetism, and on "The Wonders of the Sun." Professor Black's "Boston Stereopticon and Drummond Microscope" followed Professor Richards two weeks later. Also billed as "Three Nights of Travel and Art," Black exhibited lantern slide views of Europe and the Holy Land as Stoddard was to do years later. This Professor Black was probably James Wallace Black, one of the pioneers of aerial photography, who had taken a successful view of Boston from a balloon in 1860. Interestingly, Stoddard's earliest cityscape is a panorama of Boston taken from the top of the Bunker Hill monument; a view that approaches the lofty camera angle of the balloon pictures.[27]

As mentioned, Stoddard took part in the New York State Survey of the Adirondacks, serving as director of the Photographic Division for the 1878 season. His name appears on a list of expedition members for that year printed in the survey's seventh annual report, the only list of expedition members ever made. Verplanck Colvin, the wealthy

Albany resident who undertook the survey and won state funding for it, tended to suppress the names and contributions of associates. (His egomania turned into actual madness in late middle age.) It is possible, even probable, that Stoddard worked for the project during some of the other seasons from 1873 through the 1880s.

Stoddard probably acquired surveying skills on the 1878 expedition. In 1881 he published a map of Lake George based on "Surveys of 1880 by S. R. Stoddard." Late in life (1907–09) he brought out a hydrographic chart of Lake George made from his own topographical surveys and depth soundings of the lake. In addition to these maps, he put together a number of others using existing maps as sources – the most successful being his "Map of the Adirondacks," published first in 1880 and revised for many years thereafter.

Stoddard also experimented with new photographic techniques and equipment. For illuminating night shots, for example, he employed the recently developed magnesium flash. According to an article in the *New York Herald Tribune* of March 2, 1890 (which Stoddard clipped and saved), two Germans invented the process of "burning magnesium metal as a new source of actinic or photographic light." But Stoddard's "flash-light" photographs of two New York City monuments in the late 1880s pushed the new technology to its most successful frontier.

The Washington Memorial Arch was his first attempt, and in photographing it he came near losing his life, for the unusually large amount of magnesium metal which he employed to illuminate the subject "instead of boiling up out of the cup, as any well-mannered charge ought to have done, and as guncotton and gunpowder charges heretofore had always been in the habit of doing with me," he writes, "the force of this one seemed to be downward, like dynamite, exploding with a loud detonation, tearing the cup into fragments and boiling down over my head and shoulders in a sheet of flame that singed hair and beard, and seared my hands and the side of my face as with a hot iron; so that after I had got my slide in and saved my plate, I held an impromptu reception of policemen and a sympathizing crowd generally, followed by a free ride in an ambulance to St. Vincent. But the photograph was entirely successful."

It will be remembered how the photograph of Liberty Enlightening the World [the Statue of Liberty] was made. . . . Mr. Stoddard employed five instruments on this occasion, stationing them on the steamboat pier of the island, so that if he failed in one he would have four other chances. A wire was stretched from the torch of the big statue to the mast of a vessel a considerable distance away. Meanwhile on this wire, and controlled by a pulley, was the magnesium metal ready for flashing. An insulated copper wire extended from the magnesium compound to the electric plant on the island, so that at a given signal the electrician who had charge of the torch could turn on the current and produce a spark in the magnesium compound that would suddenly ignite it into a brilliant flash. Over a pound and a half of magnesium was used; the largest quantity that was ever employed at one time in making a photograph. . . .

A brief newspaper notice from one of the Glens Falls papers in June of 1892 describes a Stoddard-built and perhaps Stoddard-designed camera for taking huge panoramic views:

> [It] takes a photograph twenty by fifty inches, the largest in the country. The picture is taken on a curved film and with a revolving lens so that the photograph is accurate in perspective and reflective, a result which cannot be obtained in large pictures with a flat plate. This camera has been built under his personal supervision. . . .[28]

In 1882, Stoddard filed a patent for an attachment for cameras to use in dry-plate photography. Within a few years, this became the "Stoddard Combination Plate and Film Holder," manufactured and marketed, evidently without success, by E. L. Elliot & Co., Auburn, New York. Stoddard's eye for new inventions looked beyond the field of photography. In 1905, he made another patent application: for an improved trolley shoe – the device that holds the wheel of an electric trolley to the rail.[29]

The 1890s and the very first years of the twentieth century mark the era of Stoddard's travels and lectures. After Augusta Stoddard's death in 1906, he made no more journeys. In 1908, he married Emily Doty, the woman who had served him both as housekeeper and darkroom assistant since the 1870s.

With the failure of *Stoddard's Adirondack Monthly* magazine in the fall of 1908, Stoddard turned to the work of updating and reprinting his guidebooks and maps. He also produced two new maps: the hydrographic chart of Lake George, mentioned earlier, and "Auto-Road Map of the Adirondacks, the Champlain Valley, and the Hudson River," published about 1910. Perhaps his last project was a lengthy brochure and program prepared for the Warren County centennial celebration of 1912.

Dorothy Alsdorf, Saratoga County Historian, remembered Seneca Ray Stoddard from these last years of his career. As a child, she often accompanied her grandfather, George Baldwin, the proprietor of an Adirondack hotel, to Stoddard's office in Glens Falls. Baldwin stopped in to provide Stoddard with information on the hotel for the Adirondack guidebook. In Dorothy Alsdorf's memory, an extremely frail and thin Seneca Ray Stoddard gazed out at the world with intent, serious dark eyes. He always behaved in a ceremonious fashion. After gravely shaking her grandfather's hand and making some polite inquiries, he would then gravely shake her own small hand. There was an air of kindness and gentleness about the old man.

He died May 3, 1917, after an illness of almost two years that progressively robbed him of his mental abilities. After his death, Emily Doty Stoddard found that there was not enough money to bury him. The bulk of Augusta Stoddard's inheritance from her family had passed to her sons: Charles, a West Point graduate and military officer, who eventually became a lawyer in Philadelphia and New York City; and LeRoy, a Cornell Medical School graduate and plastic surgeon in New York City. The sons returned to Glens Falls to bury their father. LeRoy's wife, Alice Nielsen, a star of Victor Herbert's operettas, sang at a benefit for the burial fund. Seneca Ray Stoddard was interred at Pine View Cemetery in Glens Falls beneath a large, rough-hewn granite boulder simply marked "Stoddard."

South from Ames, North Elba

Chapter Four
LUMINISM

Before turning to look closely at Stoddard's photographs, it will be useful to consider the elusive and slightly mysterious phenomenon of luminism as a whole. In her *American Painting of the Nineteenth Century*, Barbara Novak explains that "Luminism is one of the most truly indigenous styles in the history of American art, a way of seeing so intimately related to the artist's idea of world and his relation to it that it can be identified not only in landscape painting but also in still life, genre, and portraiture."

But what is luminism, exactly? Until recently, it remained a completely unrecognized episode in the history of art. The core luminist artists, Fitz Hugh Lane, Martin Heade, John Kensett, and Sanford Gifford, were viewed simply as late Hudson River School painters, and their luminist works, dating between 1850 and 1875, looked uncomfortably like a dead end. Nothing could have been more distant from Impressionism – the eventual wave of the future in nineteenth-century painting. Instead of painting light and color playing on the surfaces of generally pleasant, everyday scenes, the luminists created silent, hard-edged, slightly surreal landscapes. These landscapes reach back to distant horizons and contain expanses of air and sky and, very often, calm, glassy water. The luminists painted these scenes as smoothly as possible, without visible brushstrokes, and gave their forms sharp, clear outlines.

Stable, horizontal compositions express something grand but also something hospitable in their views of wild and semi-wild nature along the New England coast and in the mountains of New York, Vermont, and New Hampshire.

The chief subject of the luminist landscape is light, which beams from a single strong source and fills these often austerely constructed scenes with an ecstatic radiance. In the works of some artists, Sanford Gifford in particular, the light-filled air takes on substance and becomes slightly foggy atmosphere or mist. Despite the radiance, the mood of many pictures is brooding and a little melancholy.

The classic luminist landscape exhibits features that link it with photography: a taste for exact measurement and a strong reliance on tone – dark to light values – to build the picture. It is known that Fitz Hugh Lane used the camera obscura or other photographic apparatus as a first step in some of his paintings. Frederick Church and Albert Bierstadt, less classical luminists, also employed photography (Bierstadt's two brothers were photographers), and probably others did as well. John Kensett painted a view of Lake George in 1869 that looks at least informed by photography, especially when compared with a similar Lake George view completed eleven years earlier. Since luminism's dates, 1855–75, more or less correspond with the beginnings of outdoor photography, it is likely a style that developed in tandem with the new technology. Certainly, the medium of photography favored the clean lines and hard edges of luminist scenes.

Who are the luminist photographers? Writing in his *American Light*, John Wilmerding finds "fre-quent luminist themes" in the works of all the major photographers of the West. But A. J. Russell, William Henry Jackson, Timothy O'Sullivan, and others were "by no means consistently . . . part of the movement."

Wilmerding gives consistent status to Carleton Watkins and Stoddard, along with two amateurs who worked in the Northeast, Louise Deshong Woodbridge and Henry Rand. In addition to Watkins's "classic luminist themes of still water, breathtaking vistas, and calculated spatial recession, he above all made pure, ineffable light his object of attention." On Stoddard:

Working around the Lake George area at about the time the first large tourist hotels were opening, contemporaneous with the arrival of Kensett, Heade, and other painters, Stoddard . . . here took some of the purest luminist photographs we might find.

His view of "The Horicon Sketching Club" (1882) . . . has the stillness of mood and flat balanced order of a luminist vision and, in fact, is very close to the drawings and paintings David Johnson did nearby during the same years. Other photographs at Lake George, Upper Saranac Lake, and Little Tupper Lake display various luminist qualities: horizontal order, balanced tonal contrasts, open surfaces of silvery water, and low sunlight faced centrally across the view, its reflection a vertical bar perfectly intersecting the shorelines' horizontals. [Still other] photographs draw our attention to infinitely subtle variations of hillside reflections in near-motionless water. Their balancing of silhouetted shapes, both vertically and horizontally, immediately calls to mind the oils of Lane and Kensett.

Ralph Waldo Emerson was a key intellectual source for luminism. His essay "Nature" (1836) expresses an exultant belief in the goodness, beauty, and divinity of unspoiled nature:

In the woods is perpetual youth. Within these plantations of God, a decorum and sanctity reign, a perennial festival is dressed, and the guest sees not how he should tire of them in a thousand years. In the woods we return to reason and faith. There I feel that nothing can befall me in life – no disgrace, no calamity (leaving me my eyes) which nature cannot repair. Standing on the bare ground – my head bathed by the blithe air and uplifted into infinite space – all mean egotism vanishes. I become a transparent eye-ball. I am nothing. I see all. The currents of the Universal Being circulate through me; I am part or particle of God. . . . In the wilderness, I find something more dear and connate than in streets or villages. In the tranquil landscape, and especially in the distant line of the horizon, man beholds somewhat as beautiful as his own nature.

The greatest delight which the fields and woods minister, is the suggestion of an occult relation between man and the vegetable. I am not alone and unacknowledged. They nod to me and I to them.

The "transparent eye-ball" sounds a bit like a camera. Coincidentally, Louis Daguerre took his first successful photograph a year after Emerson wrote his essay. Emerson's phrase "the distant line of the horizon" in any case evokes the luminist landscape especially.

Ideas along the lines of Emerson's had actually been occurring to numbers of thoughtful people at about this time. The painter Thomas Cole had begun painting landscape views of the American wilderness in the 1820s. He was soon followed by the loose brotherhood of New York painters known to later generations as the Hudson River School. In England, the focus on nature appeared a little earlier still, in the poetry of William Wordsworth and the landscape painting of J. M. W. Turner and John Constable. It is clearly no accident that these developments coincide with the first full impact of the industrial age in both England and America.

When Western society turned its attention to nature, scientists as well as artists and writers began to examine the natural world with new zeal. Botanists, geologists, geographers, explorers of all kinds actively gathered and classified quantities of information. Their discoveries excited the interest of average people. When the geologist Louis Agassiz visited an Adirondack village with Emerson and other notables, Agassiz was the celebrity best known to the inhabitants.[1]

The German scientist Alexander von Humboldt – author of *Cosmos*, a kind of geography and explanation of the entire world – inspired artists like Frederick Church to travel and record exotic nature. Church voyaged to South America and the Arctic to collect hundreds of detailed sketches for the panoramic landscapes he eventually presented to the public. Artists formed part of the scientific endeavor, and the line between artist and scientist was often a bit blurred. As late as the 1890s Stoddard apparently considered Edwin Peary, the arctic explorer, a colleague of sorts, a fact that surprises today. In a letter to the editor of a Glens Falls newspaper concerning a lecture by Peary, Stoddard took the stance of a senior artist/explorer reviewing the work of a junior one. He found Peary's "simple story" of value, but: "The pictures are not all perfect...."[2]

The line between art and religion was also indistinct. The writings of John Ruskin, which reached the United States in 1849, identified "the interest in art with morality and religion as well as with the love of nature." Ruskin built "a loose but convincing system where art, religion, and nature were inextricably intertwined." His observations of nature – cloud formations, plant structures, and other things – approached the scientific. He admired artists who were equally rigorous in their depictions of nature, and, early on, he looked to the invention of photography to enhance painting.

The world of learning was still a surprisingly whole place in the 1840s and 1850s, with the different branches of knowledge striving together in a common purpose. That purpose was to know the world, but also to confirm the teachings of the Old and New Testaments. But perhaps this states things wrongly. People simply expected research of all kinds to confirm religious teachings. Within a few years, when some scientific findings appeared to contradict the Bible, scholars were appalled.

In 1859 Darwin published his *Origin of Species*. After Darwin and also after the 1861–65 American Civil War, which shocked the world with its horrendous casualty rates, ideas changed. Over the course of a decade or two, artists and scientists gradually left off this pointed search for God in nature. It had

been a wonderful idea – the notion that God animated his creation in an immediate and lively way, and thus could be approached, understood, and communed with very directly. (Perhaps *easily* was also the feeling.) It is not surprising that luminism, the flowering of this belief in painting and photography, produced beautiful and compelling works.

Barbara Novak sees past specific literary sources to a deeper origin for this clear, sharp-edged, light-filled vision of the world. She finds a proto-luminist tradition in American painting, stretching from the eighteenth century's John Singleton Copley through later nineteenth-century painters such as Thomas Eakins and Winslow Homer, and even into the twentieth century in the works of Edward Hopper. Novak points to this specifically American eye as coming out of craft or primitive painting styles, which are also highly linear and subjective. But, basically, she sees the viewpoint as springing rather directly from the soul of a pragmatic, down-to-earth, but also highly religious populace. Though Emerson and his sympathizers had moved many steps away from the Puritan religion of their forefathers, they were still a very serious-minded group. Europeans picked up on the sober, spiritual quality in American luminist painting right away. Some, such as William Thackeray, didn't like it. On an 1855 visit to the United States, Thackeray met John Kensett and rated him an excellent artist, but found his "New England wood and sea shore scenery ... wan and melancholy." Thackeray wrote: "I like the English style best ... a great buxom elm tree, a jolly green sward."[3]

Several writers have investigated the similarities between luminism and seventeenth-century Dutch painting: the realism, the clarity, the interest in light. Even specific details such as a fairly low horizon (versus the higher one seen in Hudson River School paintings) and the use of the camera obscura are shared by both of these types of painting. One art historian links the aesthetic of Dutch painting specifically with that of nineteenth-century photography. Both present "a moment of time captured and held still – even as it shimmers with life and living atmosphere."[1] Whatever the case, there is little doubt that the ideas that brought forth luminist painting seemed to stimulate a similar mode of expression in certain photographers, and Seneca Ray Stoddard was one of them. Stoddard, as a photographer with a background in craft painting and a family tree packed with Calvinist (and later, Methodist) ministers, possessed natural links with some of the chief sources of luminism.

Saranac Lake, from Prospect House

St. Hubert's Isle, Raquette Lake

Owl's Head at Long Lake

Raquette Lake, at the mouth of the Marion River

Black Mountain from Lake George

Chateaugay Lake, north from Indian Point

Upper Au Sable Pond

Lake George, looking south from Mohican House

Lake George, showing Black Mountain

At Sabbath Day Point, Lake George. The man observing the scene is probably Stoddard.

Crawford Notch, in the White Mountains of New Hampshire

Chapter Five
THE SUN PICTURES

Stoddard made his photographs in the midst of a lively artistic scene. Artists swarmed to Lake George and into the Adirondacks throughout the middle and late years of the nineteenth century. In the 1850s and early 1860s, numbers of artists came directly from Albany and Troy.

The young Albany artist Edward Gay spent the summer at Lake George in 1858 as one of a "brilliant camp" of "gilded youths" who were the sons of "the old Dutch aristocrats of Albany." The camp included James Kidd, a wealthy man from Albany and an artist, as well as James Hart and Gay. Both William Hart and William Richardson Tyler visited Keene Valley in the early 1860s; there is a Hart painting, *Evening in Keene Valley*, dated 1861, and a Tyler painting, *View of Keene Valley*, dated 1865.

John A. Griswold, Troy's leading iron and steel manufacturer, vacationed in the Adirondacks during the same years. Alfred Street's *Woods and Waters on the Saranac and Racket*, first published in 1860 (nine years before W. H. Murray's *Adventures in the Wilderness*), has an 1865 edition dedicated to John A. Griswold of Troy as a "memento of friendship and the happy hours we have enjoyed with other members of the Saranac Club in the great wilderness of our native state." The edition contains "two illustrations on wood designed by William Hart."

Griswold probably commissioned the wartime picture by William Richardson Tyler *Conflict Between the "Monitor" and the "Merrimac" at Hampton Roads* (1862), because the Griswold Company built the iron-plated *Monitor*. One of the sponsors of the Troy Exhibition of 1862, Griswold owned a number of the exhibition paintings, including two Sanford Giffords.

It was not only artists with local connections, however, who came to the Adirondack region in the third quarter of the nineteenth century and beyond. The whole fellowship of Hudson River painters came. During the late 1860s and early 1870s, Stoddard painted and photographed on Lake George in company with John Kensett and his friend and student David Johnson. Stoddard's photographs of the lake from this time resemble Kensett's and Johnson's paintings. They show the same very low horizon lines and austere compositions – with volumes of empty air hanging above flat expanses of water, and with the simple forms of mountains or rocks framing the contemplative space. Stoddard photographed Sloop Island, Kensett's favorite camping ground, in this manner.

Stoddard describes his operations on Lake George in a humorous (and also self-conscious) way in his 1873 guidebook:

Jack had been staying at Fourteen Mile Island for some time … one morning after assisting in the customary duty of seeing the steamer away on her trip down the lake [he] stood gazing at a well-known sail, evidently making for the island, when he was captured and conducted mysteriously behind a tree

by Mr. Smith, who, apparently, had some weighty communication to make.

"See that boat coming out there?" he inquired evidently excited.

"I'm looking at it," said Jack. "Elegant thing, isn't it? Looks like a snow plow with a dry-goods box on the hind end."

"Exactly; couldn't describe it better myself. Sails like a stone-boat; chucks on the waves like an old pile-driver; and will go every way but straight ahead. Know that long fellow lying around loose on the 'box' trying to steer?"

"Well," said Jack, "I'm inclined to think it's Victor Hugo's devil fish, judging by the way he spreads out over the top."

"Pretty good – original idea! Well, that's Stoddard, the photographer, and that's his boat, the Wanderer. He wanders around all over the lake, taking views and money. Notice that picture on his sail, looking more like cancer in the old-fashioned almanacs than any thing else that I can think of? Well, he calls that his 'coat of arms' – legs would be more appropriate – and it is supposed to be himself astride of a camera (his hobby) in pursuit of wealth, there represented by a fat-looking money bag with wings, to show the nature of the game which he hopes to bring down by aid of his lance, that being as he also claims to be an artist, a mahl stick."

The "well-known sail" suggests that Stoddard and the *Wanderer* traveled the lake regularly and encountered many of the artists who painted there. The sole Lake George artist of the time to keep a regular diary, John Henry Hill, records a visit from

Stoddard, as well as visits from the painters David Johnson and Richard Hubbard. Hill (who was, confusingly, the son and grandson of two other John Hills, who were also artists) lived on a small island in the lake between 1870 and 1873 and worked at creating enormous canvases of western landscape which, like other artists of the day, he assembled and completed in the studio from oil sketches previously made on location. Hill aimed for photographic reality in his painting: "A friend to whom I showed the study made on the spot from which the picture [his *The Domes of Yosemite*] is painted and a photograph taken from nature said, I am astonished, they are identical. . . ." Hill chose a hermitlike existence for himself, remaining on Phantom Island through the winter. Stoddard walked over the ice to visit him in February of 1873:

> *Stoddard from Glens Falls called in the afternoon, came up to get some photographs of winter scenery on the lake and is going to have published a small guidebook of the lake and wanted to know what he was going to say about this establishment. Said there was a great deal of curiosity manifested and many enquiries made about it. Yes, thinks I, I have had a studio in Broadway and have exhibited pictures on the academy walls for a number of years and have received high commendation from most of the New York artists and from [illegible] and Ruskin and thousands of people have seen my work and precious few enquiries made about it. And now when I choose to take them at their word and cut clear of their unconcern and tend to my own business – these numbsculls [sic] are wide awake with astonishment. . . .*[1]

Hill's familiar use of the expression "Stoddard from Glens Falls," and the fact that Hill seems to view Stoddard as partly an emissary from the world of artists and patrons, speaks of numerous contacts between the photographer and painters working in the area. Stoddard surely knew the Glens Falls–born artist, Henry Augustus Ferguson, whose brother's house stood within a block of the Stoddards' on Elm Street. Ferguson appears off and on in James Smillie's diary. In September 1868 Smillie painted in the Adirondacks near Keene Valley with Ferguson, and later reported that on the trip back to New York City "Ferguson left us at Fort Edward," evidently heading to Glens Falls just a few miles distant. During this period, Ferguson occupied a studio in a building on 10th Street in New York City, where the Albany artists Homer Dodge Martin, Launt Thompson, and Eastman Johnson also had rooms, along with Sanford Gifford, Richard Hubbard, Jervis McEntee, and others.[2]

Ferguson, another painter who stepped from the regional/craft world, first trained under his brother Hiram, a wood engraver in Albany. (Ferguson may have later both elaborated and obscured his past; his obituary of 1911 in the *New York Times* states that he attended Trinity College and also that his birthdate was unknown, since the artist refused to reveal it.) In 1862, Henry Ferguson set up on his own as a landscape painter in Albany, moving to New York City in about 1865. He painted in the Adirondacks each summer at least through 1869; he produced a painting called *In Keene Valley* in 1870. During the next two decades he traveled to South America, Europe, and Mexico, creating panoramic landscapes after the manner of Frederick Church. But he came home to Glens Falls on occasion. In 1882 he painted a view of the Glens Falls bridge that resembles, but is not identical to, a Stoddard photograph taken from the same distance and angle.

In the 1870s, Stoddard specifically marketed his photographs to artists. His first edition of the *Adirondacks Illustrated* guidebook advertises: "Large views 8 × 10 and 11 × 14 . . . designed as studies for artists." A large album of photographs that Stoddard kept aboard one of the Lake George steamboats claims "100 Landscape Studies – Trees, Rocks & Cloud Effects – Designed for Artists."[3]

Curators at the Adirondack Museum have matched a landscape painting by Henry Suydam (b. 1804–d. after 1884) to a Stoddard stereograph view of Haystack Mountain. Suydam was the older brother of the more famous James Suydam, another painter, who died in 1865. (James was on a summer sketching tour in the White Mountains with Sanford Gifford, the two planning to continue on to Lake George, when James contracted dysentery and died at North Conway, New Hampshire.) The art historian John Baur labels both brothers luminists, though Henry's painting after the Stoddard photograph departs in some ways from luminism. (The work has a rather fuzzy and painterly brushstroke, for one thing, and not much focus on the sky and/or a clear source of light.) The museum dates the Suydam painting circa 1880, so it is a work of Suydam's old age.[4]

But what about Stoddard's own painting? What does it look like? Maitland De Sormo acquired more than forty paintings from Seneca Ray Stoddard's estate. He sold many of the larger ones during the

1960s and 1970s, and they have, for the most part, disappeared without a trace. Between them, the Adirondack Museum and the Chapman Museum hold the remainder of De Sormo's acquisition – about a dozen small landscapes that did not find other buyers. The Chapman Museum also owns three large portraits, and the Adirondack Museum has three additional landscapes, which museum donors originally purchased from De Sormo, plus one that came directly from the artist's great-niece.

At first glance, the museum pictures present a confusing jumble of painting styles. *The Lumberman's Dam*, titled by De Sormo, is a dark, vertically arranged landscape that follows all the conventions of romantic painting. It shows several log arches at the head of a swift stream – the log structures looking surprisingly like classical ruins. A Stoddard sketchbook, dated 1866, is completely filled with vertical landscapes of this type with one exception, a single horizontal view.

Two tiny landscape oils step away from the dark, vertical format of *The Lumberman's Dam* to express another vision: that of the earlier Hudson River painters. These scenes, *Summit Rock*, *Indian Pass*, and *Keene Valley from Baxter Mountain*, lead the viewer's eyes back to a light, glowing sky in the center distance. But the boulder-strewn foregrounds and even the mountainous backgrounds intrude upon much of the space that luminist artists reserved for light, air, and thought. It is likely that these are early paintings, for in 1869 Stoddard filled another sketchbook with drawings of Lake George that are purely luminist in their compositions. All the sketches but one are horizontal landscapes with their focus on the long, low line of the horizon and the white expanses directly above this line.

It is frustrating not to find a classically luminist painting among the museum Stoddards. *Untitled, Possibly Schroon River* comes close. This smoothly and somberly painted view of a tree-lined shore with the light of the sky reflecting from glassy, still water has many of the right elements. But, in the end, the dark foliage of the riverbank looms too largely and importantly for a luminist treatment of air and light.

Another painting, *Lake George*, exhibits a palette and a brushwork style that is strikingly similar to Kensett, Heade, or Fitz Hugh Lane (muted colors and smooth, clear-edged forms), but it is a fragment of a view, a study of trees and rocks only. Several of the small landscapes – one is dated 1870 – have the rough quality of oil sketches. One tiny (3 ¾" × 9 ½") strip of canvas recalls some of Frederick Church's oil sketches. A distant autumn shoreline makes a glowing orange line of the same hot, sunset color used frequently by Church and also by Gifford.

In a large finished painting of Keene Valley dated 1877, a substantial and very painterly foreground claims most of the interest. A man (the guide "Old Mountain Phelps") looks across the valley, but there isn't much sky for him to contemplate.

This oil painting by Stoddard, possibly of the Schroon River, was untitled.

Horizon and sky occupy rather a small area at the upper right of the painting. A black-and-white oil, *Indian Pass*, has the same busy paint plus an even smaller fragment of sky. (Monochrome oils enjoyed a spell of popularity during the 1860s and 1870s – another sign of interplay between painting and photography across these years.)

How could Stoddard lost his luminist eye by the late 1870s? He certainly experimented with a very different style of painting in the Keene Valley picture and in *Indian Pass*. It is known, however, that Stoddard ceased painting about this time, so perhaps his oil renderings of the Adirondack world did not please him as much as his photographs of the same country.

The photographs express a continuing luminist vision through the 1880s; they deal with repeated themes of solitude, contemplation, and a transfiguring light within scenes of unspoiled nature. Even when his photography becomes something else entirely, it retains traces of the order, radiance, and clarity of luminism.

How could Stoddard stamp a particular view of the world onto the slice of real life that is a photograph? To begin with, Stoddard chose and framed his shots, and with few exceptions, posed the human figures that appear within them. He also cropped his prints to refine his images – so that the 4 × 7s and 6½ × 8s vary by as much as ¾" in any dimension. He manipulated the light; first, during exposure of the plate, and then again when he made prints from the developed plate. He had the further option of toning his prints; many Stoddard prints of the 1880s glow with the warm red-brown of gold-toning.

His camera was fast enough to freeze and record wave action certainly from the early 1880s. Yet he almost always either made long exposures, which turned moving water into smooth, milky pools, or waited for periods of glasslike stillness before shooting bodies of water. The revolution of the gelatin dry plate, which boasted a much faster exposure time than the old wet-plate method, plus other conveniences, took place in 1879–80. Yet it had been possible to capture the forms of waves with the older technology. (Longer exposures gave more depth and resolution to wet-plate images.) As early as 1855, the French photographer Gustave Le Gray took views of the Mediterranean that show waves.

In addition to these manipulations, Stoddard could choose to leave the skies of his pictures unbroken fields of white, or he could add clouds. Both the early collodion wet plates and the later gelatin dry plates were oversensitive to blue, so skies ordinarily appeared blank. Photographers of the day routinely made separate exposures of clouds and printed them into other photographic subjects. Many Stoddard images exist in versions with clouds and without.

Stoddard also regularly retouched his negatives by painting directly onto them to pick out certain elements. He has highlighted the guide's boots and hat in *Absorbed* (page 131); he often enhanced the perfect circles of coach wheels; and he always repainted the campfires in the night scenes he photographed with the aid of magnesium flashes.

In the 1870s and early 1880s, Stoddard sometimes turned day into night through the use of dark filters, or by the over developing of prints. He created his moonlight scenes of Lake George in this way. The night scenes of the late 1880s were true post-sunset exposures taken with magnesium chloride flashes. (One campfire view exists as a daytime scene as well [page 97]: Stoddard simply blacked out the area around the two figures on the left, probably by painting with india ink.)

Stoddard has left a range of clues – sometimes hard to read – that point to the chronology of his work. As mentioned earlier, he numbered his images, and his numbers sometimes indicate the dating and sequence of the photographs, but the numbering is unreliable for chronology. Stoddard, for example, assigned very early numbers, under 100, to many views of Keene Valley, Indian Pass, and other Adirondack locations that he evidently rated as his most valuable images. By way of contradiction, however, some very early photographs of Luzerne appear numbered in the 900s, well past a cluster of New York City views copyrighted in 1890 and given Stoddard numbers in the 700s.

Stoddard included specific dates within the titles of only a few photographs. But his copyright dates mark solid final dates for the photographs that carry them. These copyrights are few and far between during the early years. He registered a single group of photographs in 1877, and then did not do so again until 1888. After that, he obtained copyrights yearly between 1889 and 1893, the last period in which he worked actively in the Adirondack region.

Additional confusion in dating comes from the ways in which Stoddard "signed" his works. A variety of different signatures appear along the bottom edges of some of the photographs. Several show a hand-lettered "STODDARD," whereas a printed "Stoddard Photo" and a type written "S. R. Stoddard,

Stoddard titled this photograph Absorbed. *The subject, Rob Peck, was an Adirondack craftsman, noted for making boat paddles, who also served as a guide.*

Photographer," appear to mark out early images – certainly those before 1880.

Qualities in the photographs themselves – their style, subject matter, and photographic techniques – provide the best means for separating early from later images and early from later prints. Stoddard made new prints from old glass plates throughout his working life, so an early image often appears in a later print. Through the middle 1880s, Stoddard, along with his contemporaries, employed a particular type of albumen (egg white)-coated paper that gave a print a lustrous sheen. The later albumen papers were not quite as lustrous.

Stoddard's *Lake George, Black Mountain* (page 122) typifies the Kensett-like, classic luminism of many of his early photographs. In it a tiny, solitary figure contemplates an immense vista that opens out over a smooth plane of water. In Stoddard's words: "... the body shrinks down, feeling its own littleness, the soul expands, and rising above the earth, claims kinship with its Creator. ..." While this composition has a strikingly low horizon, others of the 1870s employ one nearer the center of the picture. A second view of Black Mountain (page 118) presents an exactly doubled world in which the light of the sky reflects in the smooth water. It is a world transfigured and filled with light.

Sometimes two, three, or more persons form a group that pauses before an expanse of water and light: the two men of the beautiful *Au Sable Chasm, the Pool* (page 135), and the man (possibly Stoddard himself) and two boys in *At Sabbath Day Point, Lake George* (page 123). Oddly, even when the human figure or figures are evidently not observing the scene, as in *Upper Au Sable Pond, Adirondacks* (page 120; the guide is asleep in the boat), and *Lake George South from Mohican House* (page 121; the men on the dock face each other), the photographs generate the same mood of contemplation and radiant stillness.

This feeling pervades a number of photographs less obviously luminist in theme and composition, such as *Hulett's Landing, Lake George* (page 58-59) and *South from Ames, North Elba* (page 108-9).

Many of Stoddard's views over land rather than water date from the 1880s and they are more complex and less purely horizontal compositions (in part because of the subject matter). Some of these, such as *Crawford Notch* (page 124–25), and *Indian Pass from Lake Henderson* (page 153) dispense with the

human observer entirely. The observer is there in *The Giant, Keene Valley* (page 9), *Mount Marcy from Keene Valley* (page 8), and *The Giant from St. Hubert's Inn* (page 140). Though the sky shrinks to only a fifth part or less of the composition in some of these photographs, the light emanating from these skies and flooding deep vistas is clearly the focus and raison d'etre of each work.

A view of the Hudson shore (page 145) and a beach scene from Mount Desert Island, Maine (page 143), both probably also from the 1880s, recall the works of the Gloucester, Massachusetts, painter Fitz Hugh Lane in mood and subject matter. It would be hard to find any photographs or paintings that express a stronger sense of psychological isolation than these two Stoddards.

Stoddard took many horizontal views of sunlight beaming on still water and forming a bar of light that makes a perfect central axis to the picture. This typical theme of luminist painting appears in early photographs, as well as later ones, for example, *Owl's Head, Long Lake* (page 116), and often in a nighttime format with the sunlit scene overdeveloped to become a moonlit one (page 69).

Stoddard made many night scenes, both landscapes and (later) of groups of people. A large part of his interest must have come from his preoccupation with light generally – the night scenes offering the opportunity to reproduce a special kind of light. But his fondness for night landscapes also connects with the luminist painters' interest in evening scenes, a motif much commented upon by critics. A true evening scene, with the sun below the horizon but the sky still illuminated, was a technical impossibility for Stoddard, as it was for any photographer of the time, because of the limited range of the emulsions available. Sun was required, either in its ordinary brightness or veiled over to become the moon, for all of the landscapes.

Some Stoddard landscapes of the 1870s and 1880s are dramatic, vertical compositions that speak to the viewer very differently from the horizontal landscapes. Yet certain elements in them link up with Stoddard's other views – the milky, light-filled water of *Rainbow Falls, Au Sable Chasm* (page 137), which actually becomes light shaped into forms, and the deep recessions of another view of Au Sable Chasm (page 136).

Barbara Novak makes the point that luminist painting is classical painting with a kind of overlay (or perhaps underlay) of primitive, folk art tradition. The primitive strain favors clear, hard lines and abstract, geometric designs. Classical painting is always concerned with the creation of a deep space and very solid, three-dimensional forms. These two different artistic viewpoints fused in luminism, which also included the spiritual, yet rational, light reflected from American religious thought.

The folk art strain in Stoddard's work is revealed in his photograph of the steamer *Killoquah* (page 90), which delights in a symmetrical and linear side view of the craft, doubled in a perfect reflection from a mirrorlike lake. Two views of stagecoaches choose the same side view that exactly centers the coach in one (*Fort William Henry Hotel, Lake George* [page 78], and the coach and team in the other (page 79). A folk artist would have painted the boat and coaches in just these ways. Stoddard's photograph of Martin's

Hotel (page 95) resembles a folk art painting, as well, in its flat, abstract presentation of the building.

Other photographs show Stoddard's attraction to abstract, linear design along with construction of a deep picture space. A second view of the steamer *Killoquah* (page 91) places it at the end of a pier, which telescopes back to meet it from a darkened foreground and provided a scene of striking depth. *Hotel Champlain Dining Room* (page 99), a hotel porch (page 100), and *Presbyterian Church, Glens Falls* (page 62) all present absolutely symmetrical, head-on views of these architectural settings in which perspective lines rush toward a vanishing point. When Stoddard places people in these spaces, he arranges solid, well-lit figures in harmonious groupings. His skill in stage management resulted in some natural-looking arrangements of figures, but the men, women, and children of these photographs still resemble actors standing or sitting on well-designed stages. (See *Fort William Henry Hotel, Piazza from West* [page 101], and *"Homeward Bound," Lake George, 1879* [page 79].) This quality recalls the painting of some Italian Renaissance artists, who depicted strongly highlighted and sharp-edged figures inhabiting palazzi in which floor tiles and ceiling beams race backward at dizzying speeds. There is a similar delight in volumetric figures and perspective space.

It is not necessary, however, to look all the way back to the Italian Renaissance to find figure groups that resemble Stoddard's. The American painter Thomas Bingham painted "classical" human forms within "classical" spaces. Stoddard's view of the Fort William Henry Hotel porch and his *Adirondack Survey Party, Long Lake* (page 85) both have the look of some Bingham scenes, with their arrangements of smaller pyramids of forms within an overall larger group.

Stoddard frequently photographed strongly highlighted figures emerging from backgrounds of darkness (see *Adirondack Hunters* [page 57], *Adirondack Survey Party, Long Lake* [page 85], and *Camp Pine Knot* [page 141]), an ideal way of illustrating the heaviness and solidity of the bodies. This accounts for part of Stoddard's interest in campfire scenes. The lean-to campfire scenes achieve a far greater naturalness than those of the hotel steps and porches, although there is still a faint suggestion of posed positions. All of the campfire scenes date from 1887 or after, so none involved very long exposures. But most of the natural quality emanates from the subjects themselves, who were more at ease in their wilderness clothes than the people standing on the steps of the Fort William Henry Hotel dressed in their best.

Stoddard did not make portrait studies outside of his studio until the late 1880s. *Absorbed* (page 131), the young man reading by the fire dates from 1887. (He probably made few portraits in the studio as the only ones to survive are some of Stoddard's own family members.) One exception to this is an outdoor photograph of a sleeping baby (probably Stoddard's second son, LeRoy in a hammock), dated 1876. But there is another more interesting category of exceptions, too. The photographer made a series of large portraits of Adirondack guides about 1873, as well as an early stereograph portrait of an Indian girl, taken at Lake George. (There are several additional stereo scenes of a Lake George Indian camp.) What was it about these individuals that claimed Stoddard's attention? The Indian girl and the hermit Alvah Dunning (page 53) lived close to, actually intertwined with, the unspoiled nature Stoddard and others saw as uplifting and healing. He surely took their portraits to record some quality of the "pure" primitive hovering about their features. In his Lake George guidebook, Stoddard jokes about not finding noble qualities in the present-day Indian. But his jokes do not rule out a true disappointment on this score.

Civilized man, unlike an idealized primitive man, leaves his mark on the landscape. Trains, train tracks, and tree stumps stand as the visible symbols of encroaching civilization. Novak finds that mid-century painters incorporated these elements in landscapes with an ambivalent spirit, treating them as positive symbols of national growth and progress and also as negative symbols of civilization's trespass into the silence and holiness of "Nature's temple." This last view touches a Stoddard photograph of Blue Mountain Lake (page 142) in which prominent, jagged stumps occupy the foreground and a small party, with their backs to the viewer, gaze out over a long vista of forest and lake.

Stoddard's early photograph of a train and railway bridge also expresses this ambivalence in the face of striking change. The view makes a bold contrast between a modern railway bridge bisecting the picture from side to side with its tiny locomotive on top and an old curving roadway and gently sagging covered bridge beneath. The photographer poses old versus new so sharply that he makes it a problem or question that asks for an answer (*Bridge Across the Sacandaga at Luzerne* [page 144]).

Au Sable Chasm, the Pool

Au Sable Chasm, up from Table Rock

Rainbow Falls, Au Sable Chasm

"The Old Man of the Mountains," seen from Catskill on the Hudson River

Indian Head, Mount Desert Island, Maine

The Giant, from St. Hubert's Inn

Lean-to at Camp Pine Knot, at Raquette Lake. One of the earliest of the great camps,
Pine Knot was built by the ambitious Adirondack developer and promoter William West Durant.

Blue Mountain Lake and Ordway House from Blue Mountain

Mount Desert Island, Maine, the Green Mountain Railway

Bridge across the Sacandaga River at Luzerne

Hudson River above Thurman

Stoddard used train tracks repeatedly as an effective means of plunging the eye back from foreground to deep background (*Mount Desert Island, Green Mountain Railway* [page 143], and *Hudson River above Thurman* [page 145]). It is hard to read any sense of sadness or loss into these pictures. But here is Stoddard writing in *Adirondacks Illustrated* of 1874:

Ring up the curtain to low, sweet music, the music of a September night, the blending of the myriad voices of the swamp into one long monotone, that seems to make you, wherever you stand and listen, its center. . . . A low, rumbling sound comes from the south . . . and from out the earth, with breath of flame and eye of fire gleaming out ahead, thunders the night express. Across the marsh, it comes, bringing in its train a host of lesser lights, and with a shriek that clashes sharply and is broken into a confused din of echoes, it plunges into the northern wall, through the narrow cut to the other side, and with the hiss of escaping steam, the noisy clanging of its bell, the rattling of iron rods and links, the trembling, jerking and swaying of the long coaches, as the brakes are drawn hard against the moving wheels; then with the dying roar of its subsiding power, the iron monster rests at the end of its journey. Just for the moment we feel the hush.

The chief aim of Stoddard's photography, however – above all others – is the depiction of light. He studied and reproduced different forms of light. He follows behind the seventeenth-century Dutch painters in an attention to windows and mirrored surfaces. (*Mohican Point, Bolton-on-Lake George* [page 154], *Glass Globe at Fort William Henry Hotel* [page 96], and *Slide from Roger's Rock Hotel* [page 96]). Light shines brilliantly through the windows of the Hotel Champlain dining room (page 99) and the Glens Falls Presbyterian Church (page 62), and it floods the stairwell of the Hotel Champlain (page 155) in a distinct ray or sunburst. The cloud of sunlight in the garden of the United States Hotel, Saratoga Springs (page 157), makes another sunburst; it is a sunray entering a dark interior through a "woody" window. The clear light which picks out and outlines the forms of objects (page 77) and people (*Absorbed* [page 131]) recalls the Dutch painters, too.

The glass globes of the Lake George hotels offer only a small diversion from Stoddard's chief mirror: glassy lake water. The reflections in still, and not quite still, water are one of Stoddard's major preoccupations. He writes in his *Adirondacks Illustrated*: "the cedars that line it . . . stand at every conceivable angle with the surface of the stream . . . the whole duplicated in the mirror below, seemingly made our journey lie through grand isles of gothic arches on either side, while we floated on a thin something that held us suspended between the heavens above and the heavens below." And also: "a glittering edge of light that marked the line between the real and the reflected."

The clear light of solid forms and their reflections, as well as a foggy, diffuse radiance, exist within the same Stoddard pictures. In fact, the majority of the landscapes contain a juxtaposition of clear, sharply defined light in the fore- and middle grounds with hazy light and atmosphere in the far distance.

But sometimes sun-filled mist clouds water and air throughout a photograph. It dissolves the waterline, forming a kind of radiant wall behind the steamer *Colvin* (page 159) and the steamer *Ganouski* (page 158). Stoddard writes of seeing another steamboat, the *Vermont*, pulling away from a dock at night: "the great mass swings out into the channel, and moves away through the night like a great pearl surrounded by a luminous atmosphere." A similar wall of foggy light makes a background for the little island on which the ladies of the Horicon Sketching Club sit and draw (page 74). This light creates much of the enchanted, idyllic mood of the picture.

Sanford Gifford employed this atmospheric light, which a Gifford biographer calls "aerial luminism." Gifford visited Lake George in 1865 (right after James Suydam's death), and he produced the painting *Lake George in Autumn* the next year. He also spent August and September of 1867 in the Adirondacks with Jervis McEntee. But lesser painters active in the Adirondacks through the 1860s and 1870s, William Richardson Tyler for one, painted landscapes with the same type of radiant, veiled light. Tyler's *Landscape with Cows* in the Troy Public Library and his *Harbor Scene* in the collection of the Rennselaer County Historical Association both exhibit a kind of fogged-over sunlight that approaches Gifford's "aerial" effects.

Interestingly, Stoddard published a book of photographs with brief text, *Lake George*, in 1883 with the credit, "Artotype Illustrations by Edward Bierstadt." Bierstadt, the brother of the painter Albert Bierstadt, was also a photographer, but most of the book's illustrations are clearly Stoddard images. Bierstadt was merely responsible for the "Artotype" process printing of the photographs. Whatever the "Artotype" process involved, it produced grayed, softened, slightly veiled pictures, also very like Gifford's atmospheric style.

Stoddard created the "walls of light" in *Steamer Colvin* (page 159) and *The Horicon Sketching Club* by using long exposures; both photographs show the rather milky look of moving water, like that of smoothed-out wavelets. (The two photographs are dated 1878 and 1882, respectively.) Stoddard took pains to render smoke, mist, and atmosphere in other photographs of presumably briefer exposures. Some of these are from estimated early dates, such as *Blue Ridge from Root's* (page 41) and *The Adirondacks, View at North Elba* (page 42), and some are of late dates like *The Giant from St. Hubert's Inn* (page 140). The photographer's rendering of atmosphere was not a chance or lucky effect. He writes in *Adirondacks Illustrated*:

> *not a breath stirred the surface, nothing, save the Indian summer haze, which itself seemed luminous, dimmed the splendour of the sun's beams. . . . Indian summer had hung her mantle of haze over the great cliff and it seemed but a shade or two deeper than the blue above. . . . The eye saw it hanging in mid-air, a cloud, an outline, a color; tender, sweet, luminous. . . . Motionless, it still seemed to be sweeping grandly away as clouds shot upward from behind and passed over to the east, then approaching, and retreating, as cool gray shadows and yellow sunlight raced swiftly across or lay in slant bars along down its misty face.*

At least one contemporary, an editor of *The Philadelphia Photographer*, noted Stoddard's special attention to atmosphere. His comment comes within a longish appreciation in the June 1876 issue of the monthly magazine:

We were surprised and delighted a few days ago at receiving a collection from Mr. S. R. Stoddard of Glens Falls, N.Y. They consist of stereos, and larger views of 6 × 10 and 10 × 14 inches in size. In looking over some of the beautiful views of European scenery, by some of their best artists, we have often sighed for such work by American artists, and now we have it from Mr. Stoddard. The stereos are perfect gems of photography, including Ausable Chasm, Lake George, instantaneous and general landscape scenes. But the larger views captivate us most. They seem to be filled with the feeling and expression of the true artist. For choice of subjects, arrangement, and balance of lines, depth and beauty of perspective, well chosen and effective foregrounds, and clearly defined yet subdued distance, which with dainty skies give a charming sense of real atmosphere, we have rarely seen these views excelled.

At this time most photographers aimed for a picture that was sharply defined throughout. The editor's remark about "clearly defined yet subdued distance" makes a kind of nod to this viewpoint. In fact, a great many – perhaps the majority – of Stoddard's views don't have clear lines in the deep backgrounds. Instead, the lines dissolve in haze or light. The western photographers Watkins, Muybridge, and sometimes Jackson recorded distant mountains dissolved in mist, but all these men seem to have touched up the outlines of faraway mountains on occasion, something that Stoddard, for all his painting on of light or highlighting of figures, never did.

Frank Sutcliffe, an English photographer active from the 1880s through the first years of the twentieth century, wrote of an encounter with the English landscape photographer Francis Frith in the 1870s:

[Frith] had stretched a piece of very fine tissue paper over the back of a negative. . . . On this tissue paper Mr. Frith was working with a stump and blacklead. Now, instead of rubbing on the blacklead over the distant parts of the landscape . . . he was rubbing it on the foreground. When I ventured, with the audacity of youth, to ask whether such treatment would not make the distant hills appear nearer, and come out darker on the print, Mr. Frith said that was his intention, and then he went on to explain in the kindest possible way that the people who bought photographs preferred them with as little atmosphere as possible. After that, Mr. Frith showed me how it was possible still further to get rid of any haze or want of clearness in distant objects, by cutting pieces of tissue paper to cover the most transparent parts of the negative. . . .[5]

Sutcliffe came to abhor this process and effect; he claimed that he later employed tissue paper for the reverse objective of adding mist, atmosphere, and distance to his photographs. Sutcliffe leaned toward a school of natural photography inspired by the writing and photography of another Englishman,

Peter Henry Emerson. Emerson, who published his *Naturalistic Photography* in 1889, found sharp focus throughout a photograph unnatural and painful to the eye. He also condemned artificial, altered, or posed scenes. He photographed the landscape and country people of the East Anglia region of England without actively posing figures within his shots.

Emerson first spoke on "natural" photography in 1886. The very next year, he awarded first prize in a photography contest to an American student living in Berlin, Alfred Stieglitz. Stieglitz won with a candid photograph of a group of children laughing beside a Roman fountain. Stieglitz took more photographs like this in New York City in the 1890s; he also championed another part of Emerson's message. This was the belief that photography rated (or could rate) as an independent fine art.

As the editor of *Camera Notes* and later *Camera Work*, Stieglitz promoted the output of new, fine-art photographers who generally made pictures with a misty, out-of-focus look. Avant-garde photographs retained this superficially "Impressionist" style until 1910–12, when new modernist currents from the European art world brought a return of clarity.

How does Stoddard connect with all this? His studies of light-filled mist made in the 1870s pre-date Emerson's work. In this area, Stoddard worked ahead of his time, or at least with a richer and more varied technique than many contemporaries. In his treatment of people, Stoddard never achieves the naturalness and spontaneity of Stieglitz's *A Good Joke* – the prize-winning photograph of 1887 – though he comes rather close in the wonderful and early *The Way It Looks from the Stern Seat* (page 11).

Many of the late copyright-dated photographs (1888–91) aim for naturalness and to varying extents they succeed: *The Veteran Angler* (page 161), *Who Wouldn't Be a Boy?* (page 160–61), *The Roadside Watering Trough* (page 30), *Hunters Return to the Windsor Hotel* (page 55), *Absorbed* (page 131), and the campfire scenes. But the sentimental titles of the first two photographs named above directly oppose the spirit of Peter Henry Emerson's work. And Stoddard's instincts always veered toward the formal and the posed. This is true in the earlier photographs (the Crosbyside Dock pictures [pages 70 and 71], *The Sweeney Carry* [page 26–27], *Camp Pine Knot, Raquette Lake* [page 141], etc.), and the later ones (*The Trudeau Sanatorium Snowshoers* [page 165]). These elegant formal arrangements are sometimes a little unreal, but then the luminist landscapes are a little unreal too. The planned spacing of the figure groups on the porch of the Fort William Henry Hotel (page 101) makes an ordered vision, as pleasing as the exactly spaced trees of *Lake House Lawn; Beadleston Cottage* (page 98). Formal order is an important part of Stoddard's vision.

Sometimes Stoddard's camera recorded scenes in a way that doesn't conform with any nineteenth-century sensibility. Either the subjects themselves were too new or too impossible to fit into old ways of seeing, or else abstract forms, textures, and patterns just leapt into the camera's eye, and there perhaps, surprised the photographer himself.

The Way It Looks from the Stern Seat. (page 11) falls into the first category. There was no way to take this photograph without slicing the boat and the photographer's legs in half and presenting the unusual head-on view of the oarsman. *A "Jam" at*

Luzerne Falls (page 47) takes in an expanse of logs, tumbled together, stretching from mid-distance to foreground, the near timbers thrusting half out of the picture. These scenes forced a new photographic reality on Stoddard and on the viewers of his pictures.

Winslow Homer and Frederic Remington both worked in the Adirondacks and both created paintings influenced by photographs like these. There is no way, however, to link Homer and Stoddard beyond general Keene Valley connections. Homer accompanied an artist strongly associated with the valley, John Fitch, to the vicinity of Minerva, New York, in 1870. He returned to this area off and on through the 1890s. Homer also painted in Keene Valley itself a number of times in the mid-1870s. His *Adirondack Guide* and *Hudson River* recall *The Way It Looks from the Stern Seat.* (page 11), and *A "Jam" at Luzerne Falls.*

Frederic Remington, who painted a number of Adirondack scenes, also belonged to the American Canoe Association, which met frequently on Lake George in the 1880s. Remington's *Coming to the Call* has the same milky water and sky as an albumen print from a long-exposed glass plate negative. Its theme of real and reflected worlds is a Stoddard theme as well.

Along with other photographers working in the late nineteenth century, Stoddard supplied some new and startling perspectives in the form of aerial views, as well as exploring the impressive but more familiar format of the panorama. He made two dramatic New York City views: the Statue of Liberty (page 166) and the Battery from above (page 166–67). In contrast, his earlier panorama of Boston, *Navy Yard and East Boston from Monument* (page 168–69), fits within a midcentury tradition of city views. In the same way a landscape taken from St. Regis Mountain (page 43) follows a number of painted panoramic views made from this angle, for example, Homer Dodge Martin's *Mountain View on the Saranac* from 1868. The nineteenth century loved panoramas. In the 1850s and 1860s people paid to sit in theaters and watch what were, in effect, giant landscape paintings, with towns and cities pictured as well. Impresarios looped these great canvases into belts and then slowly cranked portions of the picture across the stage. A famous panorama of the Mississippi toured the East Coast and provided views of the river along its whole length to Easterners. A panorama of some of the Civil War battles played in Troy during the time Stoddard lived there.

Some of Stoddard's late photographs reveal an interest in abstract forms and patterns. They are something new. Did Stoddard create them out of a new, expanded vision of art and design? Or are they chance gifts from the camera's eye? See his *Mirror Lake House, Lake Placid* (page 92–93), and *Low Tide in the Basin of Mines, Nova Scotia.* (page 162).

Late in life, Stoddard adopted the style of Stieglitz's Photo-Secession group. This was the early modern group which made soft-focus, Impressionist-style prints during the 1890s and the first decade of the twentieth century. Between 1902 and 1908, Stoddard turned out a number of cyanotype prints of a new narrow dimension, approximately 2½" × 7", generally taken from old images. He softened and blurred the lines of the images and glued the prints onto textured, colored papers. He signed and dated these works in pencil directly below the bottom print edge. Though the prints are lovely, there is something artificial in his late attempt to move with the times.

Stieglitz and Stoddard lived only a few miles distant (Stieglitz summered on Lake George regularly from the 1890s until his death), and both men photographed the lake repeatedly. Stoddard's images filled the bookshops, hotel lobbies, and even the lounges of the lake steamers docked at Lake George Village from the days of Stieglitz's childhood summers there. Yet Stieglitz never spoke of this prolific photographer of the lake. Instead, he chose to remember the tintyper George Irish.

In addition to the gulf of years between Stieglitz and Stoddard, another great chasm yawned between the self-conscious practitioner of fine art and the commercial photographer. This chasm had been in the making from the first years of Stoddard's career when he complained that "among painters the photographer is looked upon as a scavenger" and "the poodelish fop and genteel counter-jumper looks down on him as a mechanic."

For a time, painter/photographers asserted photography's claims as a fine art. John Moran, the brother of the more famous painter, Thomas Moran (who accompanied Jackson on the Hayden expedition), wrote an essay in *The Philadelphia Photographer* of March 1865, which begins with fine Victorian flourish:

Although the claims of Photography to membership in the family of fine arts have often been pleaded with warmth and skill, they are still denied, the present occupants of the temple of beauty yet refusing her admission, though the capacities of the edifice are ample. . . . Of course, Photography can never claim the homage of the higher forms of art; for in the actual production of the work, the artist ceases, and the laws of nature take his place. But it is the power of seeing and deciding what shall be done, on which will depend the value and importance of any work, whether canvas or negative.

Moran, Edward Bierstadt, and his brother Charles (another photographer who exhibited at the 1876 Centennial along with Stoddard) certainly viewed themselves as artists. W. H. Jackson and A. J. Russell had the same self-identification at the beginnings of their careers, with reason: "In 1864, as practicing artist, [Jackson] opened an art gallery in Burlington, Vt."[6] And: "Russell's work includes numerous paintings – mostly landscapes and portraits – most of which are apparently lost. . . . Among the missing works are a number of vast panoramas Russell painted in Hornellsville [now Hornell], New York."[7]

From a twentieth-century vantage point, however, the art backgrounds of these two photographers shrivel almost to nothingness. For one thing, there are no painting careers like those of Russell, Jackson, or Stoddard anymore. But modern admirers of the nineteenth-century photographers are in danger of following behind the "poodelish fop and genteel counter-jumper" described by Stoddard. They underrate not only the social status of the early landscape photographers, but also their art training and backgrounds. Writings on Jackson never fail to stress his debt to Thomas Moran and Sanford Gifford, who accompanied the photographer on the western survey expeditions. These artists, it is assumed, provided the photographer with his mastery of composition. Implicit in this idea is a view of Jackson as a talented "mechanic," someone without artistic baggage.

It is sometimes noted as a curiosity that three pioneer photographers – Jackson, Stoddard, and the great portraitist and Civil War photographer Mathew Brady – were all born in the Adirondacks. Brady was born near Lake George, Jackson in Keeseville. An explanation lies in the fact that the Adirondacks lie near Troy and Albany, and both painting and sculpture bloomed in these two cities at the midpoint of the last century. Brady first studied under William Page, an artist who formed part of William and James Hart's circle in Albany during the 1850s and 1860s. Stoddard and Jackson trained with the coach painters of Troy. Though Jackson only reports on self-instruction in his autobiography, his father worked as a carriage builder; thus coach painters hovered close in Jackson's background, at the least. The abrupt withering of this upper Hudson River cradle of the arts has almost blotted out its memory. Yet tremendous energies and creative crosscurrents flowed between the workshops of the Gilbert Car factory and other such businesses, the studios of resident artists, and the annual art exhibitions of Troy and Albany at midcentury.

But if Brady, Jackson, and Stoddard came out of the same art world, each created a distinctive art from the foundations of their common tradition. Stoddard's personality and experience led him toward a vision and expression that Barbara Novak calls the "still, small voice" of nineteenth-century painting, as opposed to the "grand opera" of some of the landscapes of Church, Bierstadt, and Moran.

In contrast to the operatic landscape, luminism is classic rather than baroque, contained rather than expansive, aristocratic rather than democratic, private not public, introverted not gregarious, exploring a state of being not becoming.[5]

These words – classic, contained, aristocratic, private, introverted – speak of retreat. Are the chambers of light in Stoddard's photographs places of retreat from a modern world grown unbearable to the photographer in many ways? The pure, ordered, spirit-filled realm of the photographs offers solace to the viewer. Many of the images express a yearning tinged with sadness. Stoddard and the luminist painters explore a spiritual world that is separate from and opposed to a booming, material one. In his photographs, Stoddard endows the actual terrain of the Adirondack region with this spiritual quality.

Indian Pass, from Lake Henderson

Mohican Point at Bolton–on–Lake George

Hotel Champlain, Lake George

United States Hotel at Saratoga Springs, the cottage front

United States Hotel at Saratoga Springs, the court view

Steamer Ganouskie at Wilson House, Lake George

Steamer Colvin at Lake George

A Good Bargain

A Veteran Angler. *Weekend fishermen on the Battery in New York City*

(Left) Who Wouldn't Be a Boy. *At Lake George*

Low tide in the Basin of Mines, Nova Scotia

Suspension bridge at Riverside

West Point cadets perform a "setting up" drill.

Dr. E. L. Trudeau promoted vigorous outdoor exercise for the tuberculosis patients at his Saranac Lake sanitorium.

(Above) The Statue of Liberty, seen from the torch. (After about 1916 visitors
were not permitted to climb into the torch because it was unsafe.)

(Right) The Battery and New York Harbor, seen from the Field Building

Navy Yard and East Boston,
from the Monument

SELECT BIBLIOGRAPHY

Adirondack Museum, Blue Mountain Lake, N.Y. Seneca Ray Stoddard
    Collection (Manuscripts. Account books. Maps. Sketchbooks. Paintings.
    Photographs. Papers and correspondence of Maitland De Sormo relating
    to Stoddard). Notes of Peggy O'Brien on Henry A. Ferguson and William
    Richardson Tyler.

Austin, John. "Stoddard Family Genealogy." Glens Falls, N.Y.

Barendse, Henri. *Seneca Ray Stoddard: A Biographical Sketch.*
    Unpublished paper. Weber State University, Ogden, Utah.

Beam, Philip. *Winslow Homer at Prout's Neck.* Boston: Little, Brown &
    Co., 1966.

Burke Assessment Roll Book. Town Clerk's Office, Burke Town Hall,
    Burke, N.Y.

Burke Bicentennial History Committee. *History of Burke.* Malone, N.Y.:
    1976.

*Catalogue of the 5th Annual Art Exhibition of the Troy Young Men's
    Association at their Gallery in the Athenaeum, Troy, N.Y.* Troy, N.Y.:
    Young & Benson, 1862.

Chapman Historical Museum, Glens Falls, N.Y. Seneca Ray Stoddard
    Collection. Manuscripts. Newspaper clippings. Maps. Paintings.
    Photographs.

Child, Hamilton. *Gazetteer & Directory of Franklin & Clinton Counties
    with an Almanac for 1862–63.* Ogdensburg, N.Y.: Hamilton Child, 1862.

Coker, Richard. *Portrait of an American Painter: Edward Gay.* New York:
    Vantage Press, 1973.

Cross, Whitney. *The Social and Intellectual History of Enthusiastic Religion
    in Western New York, 1800–1850.* New York: Harper & Row, 1950.

Crowley, William. *Seneca Ray Stoddard: Adirondack Illustrator.*
    Exhibition catalogue. Adirondack Museum, Blue Mountain Lake, N.Y.
    June 15, 1981–October 15, 1982. Rome, N.Y.: Adirondack Museum &
    Canterbury Press, 1982.

De Sormo, Maitland. *Seneca Ray Stoddard: Versatile Camera Artist.* New
    York: Adirondack Yesteryears, 1972.

Emerson, Ralph Waldo. *Nature.* Facsimile of the first edition. Boston:
    Beacon Press, 1989.

Flexner, James. *That Wilder Image: The Painting of American Native
    Artists from Thomas Cole to Winslow Homer.* New York: Dover
    Publications, 1970.

Gerdts, William. *Art Across America: Two Centuries of Regional
    Paintings, 1710–1920.* New York: Abbeville Press, 1990.

Hahn, Steven, and Jonathan Prude, eds. *The Countryside in an Age of
    Capitalist Transformation.* Chapel Hill: North Carolina University
    Press, 1986.

Hayner, Rutherford. *Troy and Rennselaer County, N.Y.* New York: Lewis
    Historical Publishing Co., 1925.

Jackson, William H. *Time Exposure.* New York: G. P. Putnam & Sons, 1940.

Jussim, Estelle, and Elizabeth Lindquist-Cock. *Landscape As Photograph.*
    New Haven, Conn.: Yale University Press, 1985.

Kehne, Donna. "William and James Hart and Albany at Mid-Nineteenth
    Century." Unpublished paper. Albany Institute of History and Art,
    Albany, N.Y.

Kelly, Franklin. *Frederick Edwin Church and the National Landscape.*
    Washington, D.C.: Smithsonian Institution Press, 1988.

Letters About the Hudson River and Its Vicinity Written in 1835–37. New
    York: Freeman Hunt & Co., 1837.

Lindquist-Cock, Elizabeth. *The Influence of Photography on American
    Landscape Painting, 1839–1880.* New York: Garland & Co., 1977.

Mackintosh, Jane. "From Collodion to Kodachrome." *Adirondack Life* 27,
    no. 6 (October 1996): 22–23.

Manley, Atwood. *Frederick Remington and the North Country.* New
    York: Dutton & Co., 1980.

Naef, Weston, and James Wood. *Era of Exploration: The Rise of Landscape
    Photography in the American West 1860–1885.* Boston: Albright Knox
    Art Gallery and The Metropolitan Museum of Art, 1975.

Newhall, Beaumont. *The History of Photography.* New York: The
    Museum of Modern Art, 1964.

Newhall, Beaumont, and Diana Edkins. *William H. Jackson.* Fort Worth,
    Tex.: Amon Carter Museum of Western Art, 1974.

Novak, Barbara. *American Painting of the Nineteenth Century: Realism,*

Idealism, and the American Experience. New York: Praeger Publishers, 1969.

——. *Nature and Culture: American Landscape and Painting 1825–1875.* New York: Oxford University Press, 1980.

Records of the Town of Alford 1773–1844. Microfiche. Berkshire Athenaeum, Pittsfield, Mass.

Rorabaugh, W. J. *The Craft Apprentice: From Franklin to the Machine Age in America.* New York: Oxford University Press, 1986.

"Roswell Ray." Revolutionary War Veteran's File #W18792. National Archives, Washington, D.C.

Sanborn, Margaret. *Mark Twain: The Bachelor Years.* New York: Doubleday, 1990.

Saratoga County Deeds. Saratoga County Clerk's Office, Ballston Spa, N.Y.

Seaver, Frederick. *Historical Sketches of Franklin County and Its Several Towns with Many Short Biographies.* Albany: J. R. Lyon Co., 1918.

Smith, H. P., ed. *History of Warren County with Illustrations and Biographical Sketches of Some of Its Prominent Men and Pioneers.* Syracuse, N.Y.: D. Mason & Co., 1885.

Stebbins, Theodore. *Life and Works of Martin Johnson Heade.* New Haven, Conn.: Yale University Press, 1975.

Stein, Roger. *John Ruskin and Aesthetic Thought in America 1840–1900.* Cambridge, Mass.: Harvard University Press, 1967.

Stevens, F. H. *History of the Young Men's Association with Lists of Officers.* Troy, N.Y.: Daily Times Steam Printing House, 1869.

Stoddard, Elijah W. *Anthony Stoddard of Boston, Mass., and His Descendants: A Genealogy.* Revised and enlarged edition. New York: J. M. Bradstreet & Son, 1865. (Originally compiled by Charles Stoddard and Elijah W. Stoddard and published in 1849.)

Stoddard, Ernestine. "Stoddard Family Genealogy." Office of the Warren County Historian, Warren County Building, Glens Falls, N.Y.

Stoddard, S. R. *The Adirondacks Illustrated.* Albany: Weed, Parsons & Co., 1874.

——. *Lake George Illustrated: A Book of Today.* 1873. Reprint, Albany: Van Benthuysen & Sons, 1876.

——. *Lake George.* Glens Falls, N.Y.: [self-published], 1883.

——. *In Mediterranean Lands: The Cruise of the* Friesland *1895.* Glens Falls, N.Y.: [self- published], 1896.

——. *Stoddard's Northern Monthly* (later *Stoddard's Adirondack Monthly*). 4 vols. (May 1906–Sept. 1908). Glens Falls, N.Y.: [self-published].

Sylvester, N. B. *History of Saratoga County.* Philadelphia: Everts & Ensign, 1878.

Troy Directory for the Year 1864. Boston: Adams & Sampson, 1863.

Vanderwerker, Grace. *Historical Account of the Gansevoort, Gurn Spring, Wilton, and South Wilton, N.Y., Methodist Churches.* Hudson Falls, N.Y.: Swigert Press, 1939.

Walkowitz, Daniel. *Worker City, Company Town: Iron- and Cotton- Worker Protest in Troy and Cohoes, New York, 1855–84.* Urbana, Ill.: University of Illinois, 1978.

Weiss, Ila. *Poetic Landscape: The Art and Experience of Sanford Gifford.* Wilmington, Del.: University of Delaware Press, 1988.

Wilmerding, John. *Fitz Hugh Lane, 1804–1865, American Marine Painter.* Salem, Mass.: Essex Institute, 1964.

——. *American Light: The Luminist Movement, 1850–1875.* Princeton, N.J.: Princeton University Press, 1989.

Wilton Town Records 1834–1884. Office of the Wilton Town Historian, Town Offices, Wilton, N.Y.

CHAPTER NOTES

CHAPTER ONE

1. LeRoy Stoddard, letter dated October 1915, collection of Albert Gates, Moriah, N.Y.

2. Parley Stoddard turns up in Albany in 1863, listed in the Albany Directory as "Rev. Parley Stoddard" (*Albany Directory for the Year 1863*, Albany: Adams, Sampson & Co. and Joel Munsell, 1863). He also appears in the New York State Census of 1865, living at 50 Union Street in the city's 3rd Ward, occupation given as "Methodist Episcopal Clergyman."

3. The $1,000 figure was determined by an examination of both land purchase prices and census valuations of land and other property. In 1849 Samuel Stoddard, Jr., sold his Saratoga County land (bought from his father in 1844) for $1,400 (*Saratoga County Deeds*, Book 55, p. 294). He emigrated to Virginia, where his total property was valued at $1,000, one year later (*U.S. Census*, Prince William Co., Va.). The N.Y. Census valued John Stoddard's land at only $600 in 1850 (*U.S. Census*, Saratoga County, Town of Moreau, p. 33). However, John sold his land in Moreau's District 13 for $1,800 in 1854 (*Saratoga County Deeds*, Book 67, p. 401).

4. Squire White Papers, MSS Collection, Adirondack Museum, Blue Mountain Lake, N.Y. Squire White, who lived in Gansevoort and Moreau, has left letters and papers describing his logging operations during the 1840s and 1850s. Coincidentally, in 1868, White bought the house in Moreau where John Stoddard lived between 1854 and 1866.

5. *Will of Julia Stoddard*, Index # 039–25, Saratoga County Surrogate's Court, Ballston Spa, N.Y. *Saratoga County Civil Actions, Leah Ray v. Enoch Gurney*, 1850, Drawer A–63, Saratoga County Clerk's Office, Ballston Spa, N.Y.

6. *N.Y.S. Census of 1875*, Warren County, N.Y., Town of Queensbury, 4th Election District, House # 137. Emma Stoddard, Seneca Ray Stoddard's half sister, aged sixteen in 1875, gave Washington County, N.Y., as her place of birth.

7. *U.S. Census of 1860*, Franklin County, Town of Burke, p. 606. Charles Stoddard appears here as "George Stoddard," but Burke tax lists of that year show that "Charles Stoddard" paid tax on 100 acres of land in Lot 51 of the town (*Assessment Roll Book*, Town Clerk's Office, Burke Town Hall).

8. Ibid. Seventeen-year-old Seneca appears as "Lyman" here, but the names and ages of the other six family members, except Charles/"George," are correct.

9. The fact that, a dozen years later, Seneca Ray's brothers were living in Watervliet, Mich., suggests that the whole family settled for a time in Watervliet, N.Y., probably on Green Island (part of the town of Watervliet). See the *U.S. Census of 1880*, Berrien Co., Mich., Watervliet Township, Vol. 3, p. 21.

10. S. R. Stoddard, "The Wilderness Prison," *Troy Daily Press*, Dec. 11, 1874.

11. G. B. Warren, letter to John Kensett, dated May 9, 1860, *John Kensett Papers*, Archives of American Art (Smithsonian Institution, Washington, D.C.).

12. *Letters About the Hudson River and Its Vicinity Written in 1835–37* (New York: Freeman & Hunt & Co., 1837), pp. 80–81.

13. *Glens Falls Republican*, Mar. 3, 1865, p. 3.

14. Adolphus Stoddard (b. 1842), the son of John Stoddard; and Addison Stoddard (also b. 1842), the son of Joseph and Maria Stoddard of Glens Falls. Maria was probably a relative as she owned property directly adjacent to the Moreau property owned by John Stoddard in the 1840s and the early 1850s.

CHAPTER TWO

1. For more on the long career of Conkey, see advertisement in the *Glens Falls Republican*, Jan. 2, 1866, which refers to service of the "past four years." See also advertisement in the *Glens Falls Messenger*, Jan. 10, 1890. Quotation is from the long-running advertisement of 1866–67 in the *Messenger*.

2. Joseph Cutshall King, former director of the Chapman Historical Museum, located the 1868 photograph within the Chapman Historical Museum Collections and described it to the author. S. R. Stoddard, *The Waltonians*, photograph, dated Aug. 18, 1870, 5½" × 9¼", mounted on cardboard, # 66.20.23. Chapman Historical Museum, Glens Falls, N.Y.

3. S. R. Stoddard, *Sloop Island*, photograph, 5½" × 9⅜", mounted on cardboard, Stoddard # 44, collection of Jeffrey Adler, Salem, N.Y.

4. *Glens Falls Messenger*, Nov. 4, 1870 and Nov. 18, 1870.

5. *Glens Falls Messenger*, May 6, 1870, May 20, 1870, and Nov. 18, 1870.

6. *U.S. Census of 1870*, Warren County, N.Y., Town of Queensbury, 2nd Election District, House # 14. For portrait commissions, see S. R. Stoddard, "Temperance Notes by the Way," *Glens Falls Republican*, Mar. 1872.

7. *Stoddard & Spencer's Directory and Map of Glens Falls* (Glens Falls: A. L. Stoddard, 1874). N.Y.S. *Census of 1875*, Warren County, N.Y., Town of Queensbury, 4th Election District, House # 137.

8. S. R. Stoddard, "The Adirondacks," *Glens Falls Republican*, Oct. 1873.

9. Dorothy Norman, *Alfred Stieglitz: An American Seer* (New York: Random House, 1973), p. 21. Kathryn O'Brien, *The Great and Gracious on Millionaire's Row* (Sylvan Beach: North Country Books, 1978), pp. 202–03.

10. *Stoddard & Spencer's Directory*. U.S. *Census of 1870*, Warren County, N.Y., Town of Queensbury, 2nd Election District, House # 196.

11. N.Y.S. *Census of 1865*, Warren County, N.Y., Town of Queensbury, 4th Election District, House # 116. Stoddard appears here as "John Stoddard," but his age, twenty-one, is listed correctly. His profession "painter" has been transposed onto the Potter son listed beside him. For marriage date, see *Glens Falls Messenger*, Mar. 6, 1868. *U. S. Census of 1870*, Warren County, N.Y., Town of Queensbury, 2nd Election District, House # 14.

12. S. R. Stoddard, *Self-Portrait as a Young Man*, photograph, # 77.218.5916, Chapman Historical Museum, Glens Falls, N.Y.

CHAPTER THREE

1. S. R. Stoddard, "Rescued from Myself," *Glens Falls Republican*, Apr. 6, 1872, p.1.

2. See the "Local News" columns of the *Glens Falls Republican* for April and May of 1872 in particular. The May 21, 1872, issue contains a play on the Longfellow phrase "Lo, the poor indian," which also appears in Stoddard's *Lake George (Illustrated): A Book of Today* (Albany: Weed,

Parsons & Co., 1873), p. 35.

3. Ila Weiss, *Sanford Robinson Gifford, 1823–1880* (New York and London: Garland Publishing, 1977), p. 9. Weiss states here that Charles Gifford committed suicide. In her later *Poetic Landscape: The Art and Experience of Sanford R. Gifford* (Wilmington: University of Delaware Press, 1988), she suggests that Charles may have accidentally overdosed on chloroform.

4. Howard I. Kushner, *Self-Destruction in the Promised Land: A Psychocultural History* (New Brunswick, N.J., and London: Rutgers University Press, 1989), pp. 117–44.

5. Composite of Stoddard family photos, collection of Albert Gates, Moriah, N.Y.

6. Death Certificate of Helen A. Stoddard, Certificate # 3669, Registry of Deaths, City Hall, Glens Falls, N.Y. Typescript of obituary of Helen A. Stoddard, Stoddard Collection, Chapman Historical Museum, Glens Falls, N.Y.

7. See "Advice to Consumptives," *Troy Daily Times*, Feb. 13, 1855.

8. Verplanck Colvin, *Seventh Annual Report on the Progress of the Topographical Survey of the Adirondack Region of New York to the Year 1879* (Albany: Weed Parsons & Co., 1880), pp. 60–61.

9. S. R. Stoddard, *The Adirondacks Illustrated* (Albany: Weed Parsons & Co., 1874), p. 105.

10. Ibid., p. 60.

11. S. R. Stoddard, "John A. Carlstrom," "The Phantom Bell," *Stoddard's Adirondack Monthly*, Vol. 4 (July 1908), pp. 29–30.

12. R. M. L. Carson, "Seneca Ray Stoddard," lecture delivered before the Glens Falls Historical Association, Mar. 15, 1950 (typescript, "Stoddard" vertical file, Crandall Library, Glens Falls, N.Y.)

13. Weiss, *Sanford Robinson Gifford*, p. 9.

14. Joseph Cutshall King has described this pamphlet, which at one time was in the collection of the Chapman Historical Museum, to the author.

15. See *Aged Indian Squaw*, photograph, reproduced on p. 125 of Maitland De Sormo's *Seneca Ray Stoddard, Versatile Camera Artist* (Saranac Lake: Adirondack Yesteryears, 1972); and *The Gate of Hell*, photograph, Stoddard Collection, Chapman Historical Museum, Glens Falls, N.Y.

16. S. R. Stoddard, "Temperance Note," (see chap. 2, n. 6).

17. *Glens Falls Messenger*, Apr. 9, 1875, and Nov. 19, 1875.

18. "Scorbutic Humor," *Glens Falls Messenger*, Nov. 1873.

19. *Stoddard's Adirondack Monthly*, Vol. 4 (July 1908), p. 41.

20. Bernhard Puckhaber and Annabelle MacMillin, "J. S. Wooley, Pioneer Photographer," *The Gristmill*, vol. XII, no. 1, Winter 1978 (Ballston Spa, N.Y.: Saratoga County Historical Society).

21. R.W. B., "Canoe Cruise Through Rideau and Oneida Lakes," *The American Canoeist*, vol. 1 (June 1882), pp. 75-77.

22. S. R. Stoddard, "The Wilderness Prison," *Troy Daily Press*, Dec. 11, 1874.

23. S. R. Stoddard, "The Adirondacks–Up the Ausable–Keeseville–Red Hot Work, etc.," *Glens Falls Republican*, Oct. 1873.

24. S. R. Stoddard, "In the Beginning," *Stoddard's Northern Monthly*, Vol. 1, no. 1 (May 1906), p. 1.

25. S. R. Stoddard, "The Adirondacks" (see chap. 2, n. 8).

26. S. R. Stoddard, "In the Beginning," typescript, Stoddard Collection, Chapman Historical Museum, Glens Falls, N.Y.

27. "Science Stranger Than Magic," *Glens Falls Messenger*, Jan. 2, 1874. "Entertainments," *Glens Falls Messenger*, Jan. 16, 1874. S. R. Stoddard, *West from Bunker Hill Monument*, photograph, SRS # 1224, Stoddard Collection Chapman Historical Museum, Glens Falls, N.Y.

28. "Off for Alaska" (clipping from the summer of 1892, probably from the *Glens Falls Morning Star*), Stoddard Collection, Chapman Historical Museum, Glens Falls, N.Y.

29. U.S. Patent and brochure for "Stoddard Combination Plate and Film Holder," Box 1, Folder 5, Adirondack Museum, Blue Mountain Lake, N.Y. U.S. Patent, Mar. 14, 1905, for "new and useful improvement in Electrical Trolleys," Box 1, Folder 5, Adirondack Museum, Blue Mountain Lake, N.Y.

CHAPTER FOUR

1. Paul Jamieson, *Adirondack Pilgrimage* (Glens Falls: Adirondack Mountain Club, 1986), p. 81.

2. S. R. Stoddard, "Peary's Lecture," letter to the editor of the *Glens Falls Morning Star*, dated Jan. 20, 189[?], Stoddard Collection, Chapman Historical Museum, Glens Falls, N.Y.

3. William Makepeace Thackeray, letter quoted in *John Kensett: An American Master*, by John Driscoll and John Howat (New York:

Worcester Art Museum and W. W. Norton, 1985), p. 37.

4. Carl Chiarenza, "Notes on Aesthetic Relationships Between Seventeenth-Century Dutch Painting and Nineteenth-Century Photography," in *One Hundred Years of Photographic History: Essays in Honor of Beaumont Newhall*, ed. by Van Deren Coke (Albuquerque: University of New Mexico Press, 1975), p. 21.

CHAPTER FIVE

1. John Henry Hill, "Diary," MSS Collection, Adirondack Museum, Blue Mountain Lake, N.Y. See entries for Sept. 12, 1871, Sept. 16, 1871, and Feb. 20, 1873.

2. James Smillie, "Diaries," Archives of American Art (Smithsonian Institution, Washington, D.C.). See entry for Oct. 5, 1868. Harriet Martin, *Homer Martin, A Reminiscence* (New York: Macbeth, 1904), pp. 14-15.

3. *Lake George Steamer Album*, Collection Adirondack Museum, Blue Mountain Lake, N.Y.

4. S. R. Stoddard, *Haystack Mountain from Upper Ausable Pond* (Stoddard # 403), stereocard, P # 151176. Collection Adirondack Museum, Blue Mountain Lake, N.Y. Henry Suydam, *Sugarloaf Mountain*, c. 1880, oil on canvas, 12" x 22". Collection Adirondack Museum, Blue Mountain Lake, N.Y.

5. Frank Sutcliffe, "Photography Notes," *Yorkshire Weekly Post*, Sept. 16, 1919. Quoted in Michael Hiley, *Frank Sutcliffe: Photographer of Whitby* (Boston: David R. Godine, 1974), pp. 141–42.

6. Weiss, *Poetic Landscape*, p. 131.

7. Weston Naef and James Wood, *Era of Exploration: The Rise of Landscape Photography in the American West, 1860–1885* (Boston: Albright Knox Art Gallery and The Metropolitan Museum of Art, 1975), pp. 201–02.

8. Barbara Novak, *Nature and Culture: American Landscape and Painting, 1825–1875* (New York and Toronto: Oxford University Press, 1980), p. 32.

INDEX

PHOTOGRAPH CREDITS

Photographs on pages: 5, 6, 7, 10, 11, 14, 15, 20, 26–27, 29, 46, 49, 52–53, 53 (above), 54, 55, 56, 57, 74, 76, 78, 79, 80–81, 85 (below), 90, 91, 94, 99, 101, 114, 117, 119, 129, 136, 138, 139, 141, 155, 156, 160–61, 161 (both), 162, 163, 164, 165, and 166, courtesy the Adirondack Museum, Blue Mountain Lake, N.Y.; pages 2–3, 4, 40, 41, 42, 47, 53 (below), 58–59, 62 (above), 65, 67, 68, 69, 70, 71, 72, 73, 75, 77, 85 (above), 95, 96 (both), 97 (above), 108–9, 100, 115, 116, 118, 120, 121, 122, 123, 124–25, 131, 137, 142, 145, 153, 154, 158, and 159, courtesy the Chapman Historical Museum, Glens Falls, N.Y.; pages 30–31, 43, and 51, Albert Gates Collection, Moriah, N.Y.; pages 50, 98, 143, 157, 166–67, and 168–69, courtesy the Howard Greenberg Gallery, New York, N.Y.; pages 8, 9, 18, 45, 66, 92, 92–93, 97 (below), 135, 140, and 144, Breck Turner Collection, With Pipe and Book, Lake Placid, N.Y.; pages 12–13, 44, 48–49 (left), and 62 (below), collection the author

All photographic copying by James A. Swedberg, Long Lake, N.Y., with the exception of pp. 53, 62, 76, 108, 138, 158, and 166, by Frederic Chase Photography, Glens Falls, N.Y.

4/3/20 dt